# The Short List

In a life full of choices, there are only four that matter

## Bill Butterworth

Tyndale House Publishers, Inc.
CAROL STREAM, ILLINOIS

Visit Tyndale's exciting Web site at www.tyndale.com

*TYNDALE* and Tyndale's quill logo are registered trademarks of Tyndale House Publishers, Inc.

*The Short List: In a Life Full of Choices, There Are Only Four That Matter*

Designed by Ron Kaufmann

Published in association with the literary agency of Alive Communications, Inc., 7680 Goddard Street, Suite 200, Colorado Springs, CO 80920.

Unless otherwise indicated, all Scripture quotations are taken from the *Holy Bible*, New Living Translation, copyright © 1996, 2004, 2007 by Tyndale House Foundation. Used by permission of Tyndale House Publishers, Inc., Carol Stream, Illinois 60188. All rights reserved.

Scripture quotations marked NASB are taken from the *New American Standard Bible*®, copyright © 1960, 1962, 1963, 1968, 1971, 1972, 1973, 1975, 1977, 1995 by The Lockman Foundation. Used by permission.

Scripture quotations marked KJV are taken from *The Holy Bible*, King James Version.

---

**Library of Congress Cataloging-in-Publication Data**

Butterworth, Bill.
   The short list : in a life full of choices, there are only four that matter / Bill Butterworth.
      p. cm.
   Includes bibliographical references and index.
   ISBN-13: 978-1-4143-1566-9 (sc : alk. paper)
   ISBN-10: 1-4143-1566-X (sc : alk. paper)   1. Christian life. I. Title.
   BV4501.3.B92 2009
   248.4—dc22                                                          2008042068

---

Printed in the United States of America

15  14  13  12  11  10  09
 7   6   5   4   3   2   1

To Dad

# Table of Contents

# ACKNOWLEDGMENTS

A book is always a collaborative effort; therefore, I have many people to thank who have invested in my life. In countless ways they have made a great contribution to this book.

Don Pape stoked my creative juices for this project. I always appreciate how he listens to all my wild ideas.

The folks at Tyndale House are fantastic. It has been such an enriching experience to get to know Doug Knox, Jan Long Harris, Nancy Clausen, Sarah Atkinson, Bonne Steffen, Stephen Vosloo, Maggie Rowe, and Sharon Leavitt.

I have wonderful friends in my life. I am so grateful to people like Lee and Leslie Strobel, Joe and Molly Davis, Mike and Marcia Scott, Ron and Kay Nelson, Bob and Barb Ludwig, Gary and Linda Bender, Bob and Lori Harron, Dave and Mary Nealey, Bill and Linda Morton, Kevin and Lorelee Dodge, and Trish Guzman for their valuable contributions on a regular basis.

I meet regularly with several men's study groups that have been a help and encouragement beyond what I could write on this page. Thanks so much, guys!

Many pastors have helped me along the way with their friendship and counsel. I am grateful for Bill Hybels, Rick Warren, Kenton Beshore, Jud Wilhite, Ray Johnston, David Jeremiah, Rene Schlaepfer, John Jackson, Eric Heard, and Mike Howerton.

Our family continues to grow, and they are truly my greatest treasure. Thank you to Justin and Joy Leslie and our granddaughters Jill and Jenna; Jesse and Marisa Butterworth and our grandsons Liam and Finn; Jeffrey and Sarah Butterworth and our granddaughters Ava and Ellie; John Butterworth and his fiancée, Lisa White; and Joseph Butterworth. You bring pure joy to my life regularly.

And finally, my dear wife, Kathi. In countless ways, you live out the Short List every day of your life. I am so blessed and inspired to have you as my sweetheart.

# The Lesson from My Son's First Words

It was a warm, sunny summer day when my fourth son, Joseph, was born on August 30, 1985, in Anaheim, California. Being our fifth child, my wife, Rhonda, and I were certain he was our last. We had two middle names picked out and couldn't decide which one to give him so we decided to give him both. When Joseph Morgan Lindsey Butterworth entered the world, things were already really hopping. Five kids, nine years and under, are a handful for anyone, and our household was no exception.

In 1985 I was thirty-three years old. It's a good age . . . you're old enough to finally get some respect, yet young enough to still be filled with idealism and energy. Our family was living in southern California, having relocated there in 1981 from south Florida. We had moved in order for me to take a position as a counselor, primarily responsible for helping troubled marriages and family crises.

Four years into my life as a counselor, I decided to try my hand at writing a book. Very diligently and with a schedule that would make an accountant cheer, I systematically wrote one chapter a week for fifteen weeks until I was finished. It was a book about family life, my attempt to approach life like my writing idol, humorist Erma Bombeck, did in her books. After plenty of publishers' rejections and lots of haggling, *Peanut Butter Families*

*Stick Together: Family Life Can Be Smooth or Crunchy* was released in 1985. Suddenly I was whisked into the world of a book tour; radio, television, and newspaper interviews; and most significantly, increasing numbers of invitations to speak to various sorts of groups.

Another element of my vocational life had been a part-time speaking career. I came to California virtually unknown, but through the persistence of taking any and every opportunity given me, I was speaking on weekends at businesses, conferences, retreats, churches, PTAs, banquets, bowling alley openings, and bar mitzvahs. It was slow at first, but gradually my speaking schedule filled up. With the release of my book, I was becoming a bit in demand. Of course, this pleased me immensely.

Meanwhile, on the home front things were booming as well. That August, Joseph was born. (Anyone with lots of children can see where this story is headed.) Everything was happening at once. Five vibrant, healthy children wanted time with their dad. There's nothing wrong with that, right? It was exactly what I wanted as a child growing up with my own father. It makes perfect sense to anybody.

But my career was also starting to take off. Because the book was selling, I was being invited to speak at places where I had always hoped to be invited. In retrospect, it was a personally fulfilling time. I was educating and encouraging people all over the country. It felt good, like a calling. Yes, that was it, a calling to strengthen and encourage people all over the United States. I liked the way that sounded as it rolled off my tongue. Certainly my family was proud of my strong commitment to hard work.

Of course, the clincher to the whole deal was the money. I was being paid a good salary as a counselor. Add honorarium checks for speaking, royalty checks for writing, and checks from the sales of audio- and videotapes, and you have an enticing financial bottom line.

By mid-1986, I was awaiting the release of my second book, *My Kids Are My Best Teachers: The ABCs of Parenting*, accepting invitations to speak all over the United States and Canada, and still counseling Monday through Friday in southern California. *I'm on top of my world*, I thought. Perusing my calendar, I discovered I was booked for thirty-eight of the year's fifty-two weekends! That should have been a warning to pull in the reins. But the taste of success is intoxicating, as many of us can say from experience. It's difficult to pull away from the table when the banquet is so incredibly lavish.

At this time my typical week was comprised of a nine- or ten-hour weekday, except on Fridays, when I would leave the office earlier to catch a bus from the Disneyland Hotel to Los Angeles International Airport. Then I would board a plane to fly somewhere to speak Friday evening, all day Saturday, and Sunday morning. Late Sunday afternoon or early evening, I would board another plane for the return flight home. Back on the bus from LAX to the Magic Kingdom, I'd find my little silver Honda Civic parked at the hotel, get in, and drive to our home late Sunday evening.

Most weekends the kids would already be asleep before I arrived home. I remember feeling guilty about not being able to see them awake. But when you're on the fast track, you learn to stuff that guilt down inside, along with a mixture of other assorted emotions that would keep a therapist busy for years. To further complicate matters, as well as proving my power over guilt, I would usually arise early Monday morning in order to get to work before everyone else. In that way, I could make up the work I missed by leaving early on Friday afternoon. I felt as if I was always playing catch-up.

My busy work schedule meant that I would often go days at a time without seeing my kids. When I helped tuck them in on Thursday evenings, it often would be the last time I would see them with eyes open until our evening meal on Monday. But interestingly enough, my life never struck me as imbalanced. "This is how everybody lives," I rationalized to my wife, my friends, and myself. Down deep inside we all knew that maintaining this pace was a recipe for disaster.

Following the normal patterns of child growth and development, our newborn, Joseph, took off in the world of infants. He learned to crawl; he learned to walk—he just seemed a little slow in the talking department. His sister, Joy, and his brothers, Jesse, Jeffrey, and John, all talked by the time they reached a year old. Even after four kids, we didn't understand that kids begin talking according to their own schedules. Whereas the other four had "goo-gooed" for months, leading up to the use of actual words, Joseph was marching to his own drummer. But then, one particular day, it was as if a power switch went on in his brain. Almost as if he awoke in his crib and thought, *Today is the day I will begin to talk!*

I'll never forget it as long as I live. It was Monday evening at the dinner table. I had been on one of my weekend junkets to who knows where. I was looking forward to seeing the kids and being updated on all that was going on in their lives. We gathered at the dinner table in our regular places. Joseph was in his high chair, located right between his mother and me.

This was the moment. Suddenly deciding that today was the day for his inaugural speech, Joseph turned to his mother and broke the silence with a crystal-clear exclamation:

"Hey, Ma!"

Before we could rejoice over this major accomplishment, Joseph turned and addressed me:

"Hey, Bob!"

I felt like I had been struck by a stun gun. My son had spoken, but did he say . . . "Hey, Ma! . . . Hey, Bob!"?

His mom and I looked at one another blankly. She broke the silence by saying somewhat facetiously, "You've been on the road too much."

Returning sarcasm for sarcasm, I retorted without missing a beat, "Never mind that. . . . *Who's Bob?*" I learned there was no "Bob," but I couldn't figure out if that made it better or worse!

Dinner proceeded as usual, and I quietly listened as my older children filled me in on all the events of their lives that I was missing because I was "so successful" at my job. After the meal, with the dishes cleared and cleaned, my wife and I talked about Joseph's memorable words.

"He called me Bob," I mumbled.

"Oh, relax," she replied. "It was a very innocent thing. He doesn't think you're Bob. You're his daddy."

"But that's just the point," I countered. "I've been so busy working a forty-five to fifty-hour week, plus all those weekend trips I'm making. . . . That little guy doesn't have any reason to know that I am his daddy."

At that point in my life, I recall falling into a deep funk. I was so shaken by my son's words, I couldn't think of anything else. I couldn't focus on what was going on around me. In the midst of all that fuzziness, it was a time of deep and profound introspection.

Of course, Joseph just kept on developing in the speech department. Like most toddlers, he began to favor certain words, using them with great frequency throughout the day.

Joseph had three favorite words. If he wanted more to eat, he would simply bellow out the word "More!" If he wanted more to drink, in the same fashion he would yell, "Dink!" And, believe it or not, he began to call me "Bill!" Granted, it still wasn't "Dad," but we were moving in the right direction.

For many days I sat in my stupor at the dinner table, consumed with thoughts of how to right this wrong I had brought upon my family, while my youngest son would scream in my ear, "More dink, Bill!"

Joseph gave it his best shot. He tried every possible inflection, every possible accent. "*More* dink, Bill." "More *dink*, Bill." "More dink, *Bill!*" Nothing worked. I was tearing myself apart inside and didn't have time for anything else.

Eventually I began to verbalize some of my feelings to my wife, who was more than willing to listen to me as I wrestled with my issues.

"I'm thinking of starting a club," I rambled in a mixture of anger and sadness one night. "I'm going to call it the 'Flashlight Fathers.' It's for all those dads like me who leave for work so early each morning and come home from work so late at night that they never see their children awake. Their only contact is when they sneak into their kids' rooms while it's still dark and shine a flashlight on the faces of their little ones. Once the fathers see that each kid's breathing pattern is normal, they convince themselves that everything is all right, and they're off to work."

Once again, there was silence.

"It's a very prestigious group, the Flashlight Fathers," I went on. "Do you know why? Because we are all eminently successful not only at our jobs, but also in our parenting."

More silence.

"Think about it," I explained. "I never feel more successful as a parent than I do when I watch my child sleep. The kid doesn't mouth off, doesn't disobey, doesn't show disrespect. . . . He just lies there and breathes . . . the way so many of us think it was intended.

"Maybe it's time to rethink what I'm doing with my life," I eventually concluded.

And that is precisely what I did.

That night was an epiphany for me. No one will ever convince me that Joseph uttered innocent little gibberish to his mom and me. I believe it was the only way God could get my attention. I was so caught up in helping everybody else in the world that I thoughtlessly neglected my own family. To this day, I am so grateful to Rhonda for holding everything together and for her and the kids hanging in there with me during that difficult time.

But this led to an even greater question in my mind.

*How will my children remember me?*

Certainly they'd have agreed that Dad was a hard worker. Dad was a good provider. Maybe even that when Dad was around he was pretty fun. But what was I passing along in the greater scheme of things? What was I leaving behind?

That was the precise moment I decided I wanted to leave a legacy of lasting significance for my children and everyone who knew me.

◆◆◆◆

I began a personal search for what I considered to be the most important things in life. After all, they were the things I wanted to be remembered for. And in order for me to be remembered for these things, I needed to actually live them out while I had days left here on earth.

What are the most important things? Contrary to what today's culture tells us, they are not found in external, measurable stuff. No, the most important things are found deep inside a person. When they possess us and we possess them, they affect our lifestyle.

You and I know them as character qualities. Famous leaders are often said to have them, but they don't have sole dibs on them. You can't bid on them at an auction or buy them at your neighborhood drugstore. But ultimately, they are more valuable than money or real estate or stock portfolios or mansions or luxury cars or diamonds or anything else that a person can accumulate.

With God's help, I've recorded my personal findings on those important things in this book. It's as if God knew that I would be asking these questions before time even began, so He graciously assembled Scriptures to provide the answers I needed.

So what are the really important things in life? The answer could be a grocery list of character traits, but I have reduced it down to the Short List.

Take a look and see if you agree with my choices. Even if you don't, at least I've accomplished one thing. . . .

I've got you thinking about it.

# CHAPTER ONE

# The Lesson from Little League

One of the greatest moments for any parent is when his or her child signs up to play Little League baseball. It borders on patriotism—a love of country coupled with a love of one of its favorite pastimes. It does entail parental responsibility: a parent's commitment to his or her child is measured by that adult's ability to attend each and every one of the games, practices, and important fund-raisers. There's something about selling doughnuts, magazine subscriptions, or washing cars that says "I am a good parent." (Do you notice who is doing all the fund-raising? It's not the kids!)

More than anything, Little League is an opportunity

to show our sons and daughters how much we really love them.

For me, Little League was an opportunity for my kids to show how much they loved me.

Like many families today, we have had a Rand McNally approach to our history together. Our first three children—Joy, Jesse, and Jeffrey—were born in south Florida, while we were living just north of Miami. John and Joseph, our fourth and fifth children, were born in Anaheim, California, after we moved to Orange County.

By the time our gang hit Little League age, we were firmly entrenched in the town of Fullerton, just north of Anaheim. Joy played some Little League but gravitated more naturally to a Boys & Girls Club basketball league. She eventually grew to be six feet one inch tall in high school and played on a team that would go all the way to the California state finals.

> **For me, Little League was an opportunity for my kids to show how much they loved me.**

Jesse fell in love with baseball. As a proud member of the West Fullerton Little League, he began as a T-baller and made his way up the ranks as high as he could go.

Until he turned ten.

When Jesse was ten, we moved.

Not just down the road or a few blocks away. We moved from southern California to northern California. Earlier that year (due in great part to the "Hey, Ma! . . . Hey, Bob!" incident) I had left my job and launched my own career as a full-time speaker and writer. My wife and I quickly determined that we could live wherever we wanted as long as it was somewhat close to an airport. Real estate prices in Orange County, California, were high, so we looked around to see if there were any other places on the West Coast, preferably in California, that had more affordable housing. After a few months of searching, we found the perfect place: Grass Valley, California.

The name had nothing to do with the "medicinal" grass California is famous for and everything to do with a delightful, small, sleepy town in the foothills of the Sierra Nevada Mountains. An hour's drive northeast of Sacramento, less than two hours south of Reno and Lake Tahoe, Grass Valley was idyllic indeed. And to top things off, the town seemed to be inhabited primarily by retirees who weren't driving real estate prices sky-high.

So our baby boomer family found a house large enough for dad and mom, five children, a dog, a cat, a bird, and some fish. We bought it for less money than what we had gotten for our tiny cracker box back in Fullerton.

Of course my wife and I didn't realize we were only one of *hundreds* of baby boomer couples who discovered Grass Valley virtually at the exact same time and descended upon it. For residents who had lived in this quaint little burg for years, the changes were myriad.

Including sign-up day for Little League. For a town that had put a handful of kids on ball fields in years past, it was overwhelming when literally hundreds of kids showed up to play.

There was a great deal of learning and growing and stretching and flying-by-the-seat-of-their-pants as the league radically expanded. But one thing about Grass Valley Little League remained the same. . . .

It was Little League on a budget.

I detected it pretty much right from the start. Coaches were abundant, but playing fields were at a premium, requiring practices to be scheduled for any possible hour the sun was up and the team wasn't in school. Equipment was a little sparse, but somehow enough balls, bats, catcher's masks, chest protectors, and shin guards were provided for each team.

Jesse was relatively unscathed by Little League on a budget until the fateful day the coach made an all-important announcement: "Come early to the next practice so we can pass out the uniforms."

Ah, the uniforms. For most kids, they're the tangible connection between their Little League team and the Major League Baseball team that shares their name. In southern California, the Fullerton Little League took this connection seriously. The year Jesse played for the Fullerton Little League Dodgers, for example, he was beside himself with glee since the Dodgers were his favorite team. A "veteran" with several years under his helmet, Jesse knew that his Little League Dodgers uniform would be an *exact replica* of the uniform worn by his adult heroes. And when I use the words *exact replica*, I am not exaggerating. Many of us parents were convinced that they were actual Major League uniforms that the equipment manager at Dodger Stadium left in the dryer too long. They were that authentic looking.

Grass Valley was far removed (in more ways than just miles) from Fullerton, but my little guy didn't know that. Jesse could hardly sleep the night before the next practice. He was excited about the endless possibilities of what a Grass Valley Little League uniform might look like. Looking back, I guess I should have warned him, but frankly, even I wasn't prepared for what would be offered up as "team uniforms." It wasn't pretty.

We arrived at the practice field early and joined the scrum of excited kids swarming around the coach. The coach barked a command to his boys, our first clue to what the uniforms might look like.

"Get in a single line over here to my right, boys!" he ordered. "That's it. Everybody get in line, and I'll pass out the T-shirts!"

*T-shirts?*

The full-dress Grass Valley Little League uniform is a T-shirt?

The dawn of understanding had yet to radiate in my little boy's head. As a matter of fact, he interpreted the coach's announcement differently. With an exuberant smile, Jesse turned and gave me the "okay" sign with his thumb and forefinger. "Dad, they even give us T-shirts to

> "Dad, they even give us T-shirts to wear under our uniforms!" my son said with naive excitement.

wear under our uniforms!" he said with all the naive excitement a youngster his age could muster.

But finally the truth sank in. When Jesse put all the pieces together, he tried to stay strong, but if I recall correctly, I think his lower lip began to quiver, ever so slightly.

Yes, Little League uniform day just about reduced my son to tears.

"Can you talk to the coach, Dad?" Jesse pleaded with me, somehow hoping that my words could miraculously make more fabric appear.

"Sure, Son," I responded. I wanted Jesse to feel better; besides, I wanted an explanation too.

"Coach, can I speak with you for a second?" I asked quietly.

"Yeah, but make it quick," he growled back.

He wasn't going to make this any easier, but I courageously plunged ahead. "A T-shirt? Is that all the kids get for a uniform?"

The coach looked agitated beyond his normal agitated state and immediately became defensive. "Well, you have to go to a store and buy him a hat, but, yes, that's it for the uniform." He scowled at me and couldn't resist one last zinger. "Are you one of those new guys that moved here from southern California? One of those 'my son is used to wearing an official Major League Baseball uniform that shrunk in the dryer' kind of guys?"

It was clear to me that despite the advances since the Civil War, there were still tensions between the North and the South. I, therefore, avoided answering and slunk back to my son. "That's all they provide," I told him. As I recall, Jesse needed some time to process this major blow to his baseball career. Initially, it rattled him, but he recovered nicely.

There was another jolt ahead from Little League on a budget, however. And that jolt was headed right toward me.

It was the first game of the season. After weeks of nothing but practice, the time had come to actually play for real. My son's team looked resplendent in their official T-shirts, hats from Kmart, and assorted blue jeans, warm-up pants, and real baseball pants. One player wore a multi-colored pair of pants that looked like they came from MC Hammer's closet.

Prior to the start of the game, something transpired that I had never seen before. Honestly, I couldn't figure out what was going on. The teams were seated on their benches, the families and fans were seated on the bleachers behind home plate. The two opposing coaches, grown men dressed in jeans, golf shirts, and Kmart hats, stepped up to home plate. There they shook hands with each other and passed on encouraging words, "Let's have a good game!"

That was cool. I didn't have a problem with that custom at all. It was the next move that threw me. Once the ceremonial handshake was completed, they turned and faced us. Searching diligently throughout the crowd, they each began saying, "I'll take you" and "I'll take you, sir," while pointing to specific adults seated in the bleachers.

For some reason, this was making me nervous; I swallowed hard. *Why are they doing this?* I asked myself silently. I couldn't figure it out. "What are they doing?" I whispered quietly to my daughter and younger sons.

They responded enthusiastically. "Dad, they're picking umps!"

I let that thought settle in for a moment and then blurted out loud, "They don't have umpires?!"

"Nope," my kids replied. "They can't afford to pay 'em, so they pick 'em right out of the crowd!"

I found this revelation to be particularly disconcerting. I began to have a panic attack of personal conscience. *How can they do this?* I asked myself. *How can they put a parent in such a pressure position? We love our kids, and we want their team to win. Therefore, would we ever call our kid out if it was a close call? If I was behind the plate and my son was the batter, would I ever call a strike? Worse yet, if my son was the pitcher, would he ever throw any balls? No, they would be strikes right down the old pipeline.*

This was a horrible predicament, my own personal morality tale. For the entire next week I paced around the house, frantic about the game on Saturday. "I know they're gonna pick me. I know they're gonna pick me," I muttered, sounding the mantra of a tormented man. I had no idea how it was going to go down, but I wanted to be ready for whatever came my way.

Saturday arrived, a day that must have been prearranged by God as one when all my worst nightmares were to come to pass. We watched the teams warm up, take batting practice, take fielding practice, then take their positions on the bench. The two coaches came to home plate, shook hands, offered each other "good game" wishes, and then turned to face the crowd.

> **I had seen that finger point at me a thousand times over the last seven sleepless nights.**

"I'll take you. I'll take you, sir," they began in earnest. After they chose two fellow adults, a coach fixed his focus on me. He pointed my direction and said very clearly, "I'll take you, sir."

Fortunately, I had seen that finger point at me a thousand times over the last seven sleepless nights. Without missing a beat, I leaned forward from my seat on the bleachers and responded to the coach with unmistakable crispness.

"Ich kann nicht verstehen was mitt mir los ist, aber Mutti sind immer noch kaput, suzammen."

That's right, I answered in German. And if you don't speak German, I believe I said something like, "I cannot understand what is wrong with me but Mommy is broken, together!"

The coach looked at me like the proverbial deer in the headlights, his blank stare scaring me. Then he snapped out of it, turned ever so slightly to look at my kids and asked, "Your dad doesn't speak English?"

My kids glanced over at me with a telling look. "This is the moment we've all been waiting for our entire lives!" was my first interpretation of their expressions. Followed by "We could get him into so much trouble right now!"

I thought I saw just the slightest sly grin appear.

> **The coach looked at me like the proverbial deer in the headlights, his blank stare scaring me.**

Inside I was actually screaming, *Help me, kids! Love me, kids! Bail me out here, kids!*

Well, thankfully, my kids didn't hang me out to dry. When the coach asked them if I spoke English, they paused for maximum effect and then shrugged their shoulders, as if to say, "That's a really good question, Coach!"

The coach couldn't hold up the game any longer. "Well, kids, I can't have someone out on the field who doesn't speak English. Tell your dad we won't need him." And with that the coach began scouring for another adult in the crowd.

I was free from my moral quandary! Actually, I was off the hook, not only for that game, but for the entire season! Of course, my poor kids were interrogated by their friends and classmates. "Your dad doesn't speak English? What does he do for a living?" To which they would honestly reply, "He's a speaker."

Yes, my kids showed a lot of loyalty on that sunny Saturday, as well as a lot of concern and compassion for their old man. Let me add that I definitely don't condone lying as a way to get out of anything. My quick thinking in German wasn't the best example to set for my kids. But despite my ill-advised scheme, they taught me a lesson that day—choices are a part of how we love.

## THE FIRST IMPORTANT THING:

# Love

The premise of this book is that we need to focus our thinking on what is really important in life. I'm suggesting that we zero in on the area of character qualities, and I have chosen four traits for us to look at. There's nothing profound about the number four, other than the fact it is much more manageable than a list of eleven, seventeen, or thirty-three. Plus, I really like golf, and when I swing a golf club, everyone I'm playing with reminds me that *fore* is a good word to be aware of.

The list of four isn't in any particular order with the exception of number one. Number one is number one for a reason. The reason is quite simple—God lists it as number one: *love*.

Ah, love. Because I'm a baby boomer/child of the sixties, whenever I hear the word *love*, it splatters on my mind like the rainbow of colors on a tie-dyed T-shirt. Let's face it—people around us have a much different view of love than God has.

In the world of music, the Beatles told us that "all you need is love." Stephen Stills implored, "If you can't be with the one you love, honey, love the one you're with." We were encouraged to get a seat on "the love train." We never had to refer to *Webster's* for the definition of the word because even that was given to us: "Love means never having to say you're sorry."

Many of us have had a bulk of our lives bookended by two television sitcoms: *I Love Lucy* and *Everybody Loves Raymond*. In between those, we made the *Love Connection* and booked a weekly cruise on *The Love Boat*.

But did all that viewing and listening about love accurately measure the parameters of love?

No. God sees love through a very different set of lenses, so we owe it to ourselves to see how He views it and how we can put that type of love into practice in our everyday lives.

Ask Christians what biblical text best addresses love, and most folks quickly turn to 1 Corinthians 13 without blinking. First Corinthians 13 is the definitive text hands down, and we will mine some of its riches in this chapter. But I want to begin with a different passage, a fresh take on our discussion.

Before the apostle Paul penned the poetic words of
1 Corinthians 13, he wrote letters to another church—
this one in the city of Thessalonica. Biblical scholars date
this as the second of Paul's letters, the first one being the
book of Galatians.

The tone the letter takes with the
Thessalonians varies significantly from that
taken with the Corinthians. The believers
in Corinth were struggling with some serious issues that Paul needed to address;
because of some of their behavior and
misbehavior, Paul also needed to dole out
some harsh scolding. Overall, the tone of
that book is pretty intense. All one needs
to do is think about the environment sur-
rounding the city of Corinth to get the big picture. Going
to extremes was pretty much the norm in Corinth, where
sins of every type ran rampant. The Temple of Aphrodite in
Corinth was home to a thousand prostitutes. Corinth was
also home to the worship of Apollo, the Greek god. As a
seminary professor of mine put it, "Corinth was noted for
everything sinful."

> **God sees love through a very different set of lenses than society does.**

Not so with Thessalonica. In 1 Thessalonians Paul's
encouragement to those believers comes through from
beginning to end. Unlike the Corinthians, the Thessalonian believers were not messing up their lives through a
series of doctrinal disasters or moral mix-ups. They were
living the way God wanted them to. The apostle Paul

> **The Thessalonian believers had made a radical commitment to Christ, and they worked hard to put their faith to work.**

writes to say, "Keep doing what you're doing!" Many have speculated that part of the reason the Thessalonian believers were following the Lord more consistently is because their church was made up of people who came out of pagan religions rather than the Jewish faith. In many ways, they had made a more radical commitment to Christ, and they worked hard to follow through by putting their faith to work.

More than halfway through his motivational speech, Paul uncovers something these believers know all about:

> But we don't need to write to you about the importance of loving each other, for God himself has taught you to love one another. Indeed, you already show your love for all the believers throughout Macedonia. Even so, dear brothers and sisters, we urge you to love them even more. Make it your goal to live a quiet life, minding your own business and working with your hands, just as we instructed you before. Then people who are not Christians will respect the way you live, and you will not need to depend on others.
>
> 1 THESSALONIANS 4:9-12

No matter what these people were doing, they demonstrated love to those around them. Looking at this paragraph carefully, we can find at least three secrets that a loving person knows. These folks were the real deal, so let's learn from them.

Here's the first important thing that a loving person knows.

### *A Loving Person Knows That Love Is the Top Priority*
Right off the bat, Paul affirms the Thessalonians' lifestyle of love:

> But we don't need to write to you about the importance of loving each other, for God himself has taught you to love one another.   1 THESSALONIANS 4:9

I get a kick out of how Paul makes his point. He's essentially saying, "Here is a verse in the Bible that really doesn't even need to be here!" Back in my seminary days, I would have screamed with delight if that sentiment had been true! Painstakingly translating verse after verse from the first-century Greek to the modern English, I would have been ecstatic to skip verses!

But let's get serious. The reason Paul says the verse doesn't even need to be there is because the love in these believers' lives was so firmly in place. Paul practically shouts, "Love—it's so obvious in your lives—it's as plain as the nose on your face!" Their lives were so drenched in love that it was obvious to everyone who saw them.

Throughout the New Testament, the concept of love always gets the highest marks. There is no character trait more important to our lives than love. Referring back to 1 Corinthians 13, Paul states this truth with unmistakable clarity.

Three things will last forever—faith, hope, and love—and the greatest of these is love.   1 CORINTHIANS 13:13

I imagine Paul sitting in one of those comfy chairs at Starbucks sipping his no foam, nonfat, sugar-free caramel macchiato. I say, "Paul, I consider you to be a godly man, someone who knows what it takes to follow Jesus. So let me ask you, what are the most valuable character qualities I can demonstrate in my life and pass on to my children?"

I'm certain Paul would say, "Bill, that's a no-brainer. The top three—the gold, silver, and bronze of character qualities—are faith, hope, and love."

> **There is no character trait more important to our lives than love.**

And before I can even respond, he would hastily add, "And I can also tell you which one wins the gold medal—it's love."

The cynic in me immediately thinks, *Yeah, easy for you to say.* I have been around Christians all my life and I have to admit, based on the things I have seen, I would have answered the question differently. Let me explain.

Let's imagine another scenario: I have been invited to be a contestant on *Who Wants to Be a Millionaire?* I made it through all the preliminary contestant rounds and now I'm seated across the table from Regis Philbin. He has a stack of questions ready, and as long as I answer correctly, I will work my way up to the one-million-dollar grand prize. Because I am brilliant (this is my imagination at work here), I breeze through the smaller denomination trivia and await the ultimate words from Regis's mouth.

"Bill, here's your million-dollar question: Based on the Christians you have known, which of these characteristics is the greatest?

Faith
Hope
Love
Pizza."

Of course I know what answer is completely bogus. "Well, I know it isn't D," I say quickly. Regis gives me a grin that says I'm on the right track.

I think about this a little more deeply and then respond, "I think the answer is A—*faith*."

"You do?" Regis asks.

"Yes, I do. For Christians, our faith is our distinctive," I explain. "It's what distinguishes us from all the other religions. We build our lives on our faith. It has to be the right answer."

"Is that your final answer?" Regis delivers his signature line.

I can tell by the way he poses his question that my

answer is not correct. So I keep thinking. "I think I will change my answer to B—*hope*."

"Hope," Regis repeats.

"Yes," I reply, my commitment to this answer growing. "In the New Testament, hope literally means 'joyful anticipation.' We have so much to look forward to as Christians. Jesus Christ is the only 'religious leader' who is alive! All the other ones are dead. I think hope is a good answer. That's what I am going to go with."

"Is that your final answer?"

Once again, Regis drops a tiny bit of doubt in my mind.

I pause to regroup. All that's left is one option. So meekly, I change my answer once again. "I think I'm going to change my answer to C—*love*."

"Love?" Regis responds quizzically. "Bill, what would make you choose that answer?"

In front of Regis and millions of television viewers, I opt for honesty and sheepishly admit, "Because it's the only answer left."

Deep inside, I try to think of Christians I have known who have displayed love on a regular basis, and I am hard-pressed to come up with a list. Instead of love, there has been bickering, arguing, backbiting, gossiping, deceit, even church splits. It doesn't speak well for the church as a whole, but it does reflect my own personal experience. Whether or not it has been your personal experience, I don't think it's harshly characterizing the Christian community. Rather I consider it a wake-up call to evaluate where love is on our individual and collective list and move it to the top spot. It's following the example of the Thessalonians.

Paul saw that love and was the recipient of it. He knew love was the number one quality that permeated their lives.

So why aren't we living lives that naturally demonstrate that kind of love? Part of the answer lies in the fact that we define love the way the culture does rather than the way God does. Society's idea of love falls painfully short of the real meaning.

If we are going to view love as God views love, we need to grasp the fact that love is an act of the will. Love is a choice. Love is volitional. God has given us the power to love the unlovable.

Do you have someone in your life right now whom you would describe as "unlovable"? You might not tell the person to his or her face, but you struggle with how to be a loving person to someone who refuses to return love. What do you do with a person like that?

> **Love is a choice. Love is volitional. God has given us the power to love the unlovable.**

For years I have spoken to groups of parents stressing how important it is to me—and them—to make the deliberate choice to love our kids, even when they are in those unlovable stages of life. Looking back, it was pretty one-sided as I told story after story of how I chose to love my two-year-old terrors through their "No" stage, or how I chose to love my teenagers through their turbulent adolescences. It never even dawned on me that my kids had a choice to exercise the same option to love me!

Whenever I think of my kids choosing to love me, I think back to the most painful time in my adult life. I went through a divorce more than fifteen years ago, and as any single parent will tell you, it is a real test of your character. I recall the days when I was living as a single dad, trying valiantly to keep a career in place while attempting to raise my five children well. Some days I felt like I did okay, other days I seemed to be able to recall only my failures. When Joseph, my youngest, was in elementary school, I remember putting together a list of occasions when love was his only option. I had recently discovered how often my kids had to choose to love me, even when I was unlovable, so I thought jotting down a list would be a good exercise for me. He had to love the unlovable—and that was me! This list is far from exhaustive, but it gives you some idea of the kinds of issues this dear little guy had to deal with:

- I choose to love you, Dad, even when you cook a meal I don't like!
- I choose to love you, Dad, even when you mix me up with one of your other children and go to the wrong soccer field to pick me up after practice.
- I choose to love you, Dad, even when you have the television remote and we end up watching CNN, or even worse, C-SPAN.

- I choose to love you, Dad, even when you make me clean up my room before we can have fun together.
- I choose to love you, Dad, even when your idea of fun is weed whacking the yard.
- I choose to love you, Dad, even when you make us go to the early church service so we can get home in time for the first NFL game of the day at 10 a.m., Pacific daylight time.
- I choose to love you, Dad, even if you are the only one in the whole room who thinks you are dressed cool.
- I choose to love you, Dad, even if your idea of "on the edge" contemporary music is James Taylor.
- I choose to love you, Dad, even if you don't appreciate my creative use of your tools.
- I choose to love you, Dad, even if you lecture me and say, "This hurts me more than it hurts you" and I have trouble believing you.

So how do you love an unlovable person? You choose to! Even when it's difficult, it's not impossible.

The apostle John put it this way in his first epistle:

> Dear friends, let us continue to love one another, for love comes from God. Anyone who loves is a child of God and knows God.   1 JOHN 4:7

Three simple words . . . *love one another*. It's not a suggestion or a warm, fuzzy sentiment. It is God's command to us.

As best as I can tell from reading Scripture, God never asks His children to create an emotion on demand. For example, God never says, "Cry, My children!" expecting us instantly to begin sobbing (though actors are paid big money to do just that). God doesn't work that way. The same is true when God commands us to love one another: often we must decisively will ourselves to do it. We determine we will love another person, even if that individual is unlovable.

As we continue to unravel the passage of Scripture from 1 Thessalonians, it's evident that practice is a key to having a loving attitude in every situation.

### A Loving Person Knows That Love Takes Practice

Take a look at what Paul says next:

> Indeed, you already show your love for all the believers throughout Macedonia. Even so, dear brothers and sisters, we urge you to love them even more.
>
> 1 THESSALONIANS 4:10

What the New Living Translation describes as "show your love," the New American Standard translates as "for indeed you do practice it." I like the concept of practice. This verse indicates that love is not something I can ever master or bring to a point of perfection so that I don't need to work on it anymore. No, learning to love is not only a process but also an opportunity for a lifetime. I will never have it down cold in this world. I will always need pointers on how to improve, so I will always look for moments to practice showing love.

Think of it in terms of a professional athlete who is out there putting his body through rigorous training every day to perfect his skills. Or how about a concert pianist? She doesn't show up to play at a concert without putting in hours and hours of rehearsal time in order to wow the audience. So it is with love. We need to continually work on loving those around us for our entire lives.

In verse 10 of this chapter Paul commends the Thessalonian believers for showing their love to "all the believers throughout Macedonia." Paul is talking about love in the context of a relationship. It makes sense that our loving acts are to be directed to people around us, most specifically to those with whom we have a relationship.

> **Learning to love is not only a process but also an opportunity for a lifetime.**

Remember when the popular bumper sticker "Practice random acts of kindness" was getting a lot of attention? I get the sentiment—it's good to treat all people nicely. But the random part always conjures up the image of a garden hose that has been turned on full blast without anyone holding on to it. The hose flails all over the place, with no direction or target in mind.

Paul says that our love has a target. Love is more than a sentimental reaction, dousing people like a garden hose run amok. Love is a series of intentional acts toward people with whom we have a relationship. To the Thessalonians, it was the believers throughout Macedonia.

This idea of love in a relationship is not what was called "free love" in the sixties or what today is called "hooking up." The physical acts of love, consummated in full sexual expression, were designed by God to flow out of a love relationship called marriage. Ask anyone who has a little time to reflect on past indiscretions. A one-night stand, sleeping around, hooking up, whatever you call it, leaves a person feeling very empty without the context of a loving relationship.

A second thing Paul mentions in verse 10 is that love is never stagnant. "We urge you to love them even more" is Paul's admonition. In other words, as amazing as the Thessalonian believers were in their ability to love each other, the word from their mentor Paul is "Keep going!" Are you feeling pretty embarrassed about your ability to love those around you? God says don't be discouraged, just practice more acts of love. Are you feeling like you've got this love thing down cold? God says don't get cocky about it, just practice more acts of love. Wherever you are on the love chart, you can always improve. And of course, that holds true for any character quality in our lives.

But Paul doesn't stop there.

### A Loving Person Knows That Love Has Tremendous Power

Part of the motivation to be a loving person is the biblical teaching that loving people demonstrate great power in their loving behavior. In most contexts, love seems to be pitted opposite power, but the Scriptures teach a broader view.

King David put power and love together when he wrote in one of his psalms:

> Power, O God, belongs to you;
> unfailing love, O Lord, is yours.
> PSALM 62:11-12

Paul knew about it, too. Let's look at verses 11 and 12 of 1 Thessalonians 4:

> Make it your goal to live a quiet life, minding your own business and working with your hands, just as we instructed you before. Then people who are not Christians will respect the way you live, and you will not need to depend on others.   1 THESSALONIANS 4:11-12

At first glance, it seems as if Paul is changing the subject in these two verses, leaving the topic of love behind. But this is not the case. In many translations, verses 9–12 comprise one paragraph. I believe this is accurate. Think back to your English teacher explaining how to write a theme paper. To do it correctly, each paragraph contains a topic sentence and all the sentences in that paragraph relate back to the topic sentence.

I believe the same is true of this passage from Paul. Verse 9 states the topic—"the importance of loving each other"—

and verses 11 and 12 elaborate on that topic. Yet neither verse actually has the word *love* in it. What's the connection?

First, verse 11 begins with the exhortation to "make it your goal to live a *quiet* life." That's a nice sentiment, but what does it really mean? The key is in understanding the word that is translated "quiet." When I think of quiet, I automatically think "opposite of noisy." That's not the meaning here.

A mother speaking first-century Greek would not use this word to get her teenage son to reduce the decibels coming from his bedroom while he was supposed to be doing his homework. No, she would use another Greek word for that sort of quiet. The Greek word here is *hesy-chazein*, meaning to be "settled" or "restful." If we were to give it a more modern-day spin, I think Paul would be saying, "Make it your goal to live a stress-free life."

This might be where you say, "How am I supposed to do that?" After all, the goal of living a stress-free life follows a stress-filled goal: love unlovable people.

How in the world are you ever going to reach those two goals? They seem bigger than life. Well, in a way, they are, because in order to accomplish them, you are going to need superhuman strength. That's where love comes in. Verse 12 reveals what happens:

> Then people who are not Christians will respect the way
> you live, and you will not need to depend on others.
> 1 THESSALONIANS 4:12

What is it that people—especially non-Christians—will see that makes them respect us? Love, of course.

I think I can summarize this paragraph with one sentence: *Love will be our definitive mark.*

People who are not in a relationship with the Lord will see something different in people who do know Him. As a result of that difference, they will have greater respect for us and greater interest in knowing the one who has caused this change in our lives.

But there's another important truth to bring up, something you may have already been thinking about. In New Testament Greek there is more than one word for *love*. In the first century, when people were describing a loving friendship that was brotherly in nature, they used the word *phileo*. (That is the root word for *Philadelphia*, which is why it is called the "city of brotherly love.") If a Greek was referring to the physical act of human love, the word *eros* was used, which is where we get the word *erotic*. But there is also a word for love that comes solely from God—*agape*.

Therefore, when Paul refers to a lifestyle characterized by love here, he isn't referring to a friendly love or an intimate physical love. He is talking about God's love.

The Lord Jesus Himself referred to this truth on the last night of His life on earth. The apostle John records His words:

> So now I am giving you a new commandment: Love each other. Just as I have loved you, you should love each other.

> Your love for one another will prove to the world that you
> are my disciples.   JOHN 13:34-35

I am consistently amazed at this scenario. It is literally Jesus' last night on earth, and He is addressing His lieutenants, if you will. The general is giving final orders to be carried out upon His departure. And what does He say? "This is how people will know that you are connected to Me."

Thinking back to the little fantasy game of *Who Wants to Be a Millionaire?* would "love" have been your final answer to the question "How will people know that I am connected to Christ?"

> **How will
> people know
> that I am a true
> Christ follower?
> By my love!**

Doesn't it make more sense to say people will know I am a Christian—connected to Christ—because of my faith? Or because I have hope? Or integrity? Or honesty?

How will people know that I am a true Christ follower? By my love! And what does that love look like? It is a supernatural gift from God Himself! I can't love my way through the many issues that face me by myself, but God can work within me.

Do you get it? How will I be able to love an unlovable person? I won't—but God's agape love will be able to love through me. How will I be able to live a life with less stress? I won't—but God, though the power of His agape love, will give me the clarity of mind, the settled feeling I need to make the right decisions that keep me from caving in under life's anxieties.

So much of the Christian life is about surrender. As I surrender my life, my will, all of me to the control of the Holy Spirit who lives within me, I live a life of power, a life of victory, a life of love instead of a powerless, defeated, and loveless life.

And that's good news. If I truly believe God's Word, which says that love is the most important thing—that it's number one on my Short List—then I have some rearranging to do in my priorities and schedule so that I really am reflecting the love of God to everyone around me. Not only will this provide a rich legacy for those who follow me, but it also makes my life stand out right now in my everyday activities.

I will strive to make love my top priority. Not second, third, or fourth—first. And as I commit to practicing it every day, love will "excel still more" (1 Thessalonians 4:10, NASB). I know I will never be perfect, but I can always improve. I will learn and grow and mature in my loving ways.

To use a golf analogy, tapping into love's tremendous power is like a smooth golf swing—you allow the golf club to do the work instead of swinging so hard you hurt yourself! God has commanded me to be a loving person, but He has not left

> **God has commanded me to be a loving person, but He has not left me out in the cold without resources.**

me out in the cold without resources. Thanks to the Holy Spirit who lives inside all true believers, I have the power source I need to be a genuine, godly lover.

Above all else, that kind of love is what I want to leave behind.

# CHAPTER TWO

# The Lesson from Fourth Period Chemistry

For some reason, school was always a struggle for me. My teachers told me I was smart enough, but I constantly failed to apply myself. I can still recall one particular elementary school teacher who circled in red ink a specific phrase found on the back of the preprinted portion of the always-dreaded report card: *Does not work up to capacity.*

That phrase became a self-fulfilling prophecy as I entered junior high and high school. Grades nine through twelve were challenging enough without adding classes, tests, term papers, and homework to the mix. It was almost more than I could handle. I was definitely in need of assistance.

I was an equal opportunity employer when it came to

making low grades. The subject didn't matter, though in the art of flunkdom, I had a special place in my heart for math and science. Today, I can add, subtract, and multiply, but divide? Let's not go there. And anything that has to do with science? My three-year-old granddaughter already knows more science than I do.

Which brings me to high school chemistry. My first high school science class was biology in ninth grade, which I somehow passed by the skin of my dissected frog. In tenth grade, I was required to take chemistry because I was on a college prep track. My chemistry teacher was more of a chemist than a teacher. Brilliant, but lacking the skills to pass it along, pedagogically speaking. This flaw, coupled with his testing method, made fourth period fascinating.

A couple of weeks into the new school year, we were scheduled for our first chemistry test. I made an attempt to study, but almost from day one, I knew I was in way over my head. I walked into chemistry lab on test day a defeated man. Taking my seat at my assigned lab table (which I had nicknamed "The Periodic Table"), I waited anxiously with my fellow students for the teacher to pass out the exam. He methodically walked around the classroom, passing out the stapled papers to each student. The pages were still wet and fresh from the mimeograph machine. Like a rehearsed ensemble, each of us lifted the pages to our noses and breathed deeply, inhaling the aroma of the ink we called purple passion.

Once we had our olfactory fix, we looked at the test.

Nothing seemed out of the ordinary; everything was straightforward. Thirty multiple-choice questions.

But then the teacher announced, "Class, can you all take a minute to skim through the thirty questions before you?" Dutifully, we obeyed. "As you look over the test, does anyone have any questions?" he continued. We sat in silence. No, no one had any questions. "Well, then, that's fine," he said. Suddenly, without warning, he gathered up all his belongings, placed them in a well-worn leather satchel, tucked the satchel under his arm, strode over to the door, and said before he exited, "If anyone needs me, I will be down in the faculty lounge." Talk about a surprise.

We all sat there in stunned disbelief. Did our teacher just leave us alone to take a test? Mind you, this was not some private Christian academy—this was a Philadelphia public school! There were no surveillance cameras or any kind of educational bugging device. We were truly left on our own, with nothing to guide our actions except our personal integrity.

**We all sat there in stunned disbelief. Did our teacher just leave us alone to take a test?**

I am happy to report that there was absolutely no cheating . . . on that first test.

But a few weeks later we faced the same moral dilemma—thirty multiple-choice questions and a teacher in the faculty lounge. As I looked around the class, I observed some wandering eyes, some neighbor nudging, some hand signals that definitely weren't bunt signs. Yet the activity seemed to be randomly scattered here and there.

Then came the third test.

It started out the same. We took our seats, received the exam, smelled it, skimmed it, and then bid adieu to the teacher. But this time, as soon as our teacher left, a student jumped on top of a lab table. I honestly can't remember his name, but from that day forward he became known as Student Leader Cheater.

"Okay, everyone, listen up," he began. "If we get organized here, we can get this thing finished pretty quickly."

I gazed at him in awe and admiration.

"So are we ready?" he asked. "Who has the answer to question number one?"

His audacious, in-your-face approach to cheating sent a shock wave through our systems. After a brief hesitation, a girl two lab tables behind me whispered, "It's B."

"Great!" Student Leader Cheater practically cheered. "It's B. Everyone write down B. Who knows the answer to number two?"

"D," said a geek in the front row, his braces glinting in a silver smile.

"Wonderful. Everyone write down D. Who has number three?" Suddenly our leader interrupted himself. "Some of you need to work ahead if we're going to get all thirty done."

And that's exactly what we did.

Halfway through the questions, a new strategy was

introduced. "So who has the answer to number eighteen?" Student Leader Cheater asked.

"It's C," answered a student.

"All right, it's C," repeated our leader. "Everyone write down—" and then he stopped short. "Wait everybody," he instructed. "If we all ace this test, the teacher is probably gonna get suspicious."

That made perfect sense.

"But if we miss one, he won't suspect anything."

Brilliant!

"Okay, the correct answer to number eighteen is C, so everyone write down A. We'll throw him off!"

Like obedient (and dumb) sheep, we did as we were told by our shepherd.

> "Wait everybody. If we all ace this test, the teacher is probably gonna get suspicious."

The next day in chemistry class, the teacher had our graded papers in hand. Imagine our surprise when he proclaimed, "Guess what, class? You all got the same grade on your test!"

We all put on the astonished looks that we had practiced diligently in the bathroom mirror at home the night before.

"And guess what else?" he went on. "You all missed the same question!"

He had a strange look of satisfaction on his face as he asked us to open our textbooks to chapter 4.

"Wow, you are amazing!" I said to Student Leader Cheater in the hallway after class. "That was pretty gutsy."

"It's a gift," he replied humbly, as if he were burdened with this blessing that needed to be passed along to those less academically inclined.

Suddenly I had an idea. "Can you do this in other subjects too?" I blurted out excitedly.

"Well, yes," he replied. "Where do you need help?"

"German," I said. "Every Friday we have to conjugate a list of German verbs—you know, *ich habe, du hast, er hat, wir haben, ihr habt, sie haben.* I just can't memorize them."

"Hmm." Student Leader Cheater thought carefully for a moment and then said, "It sounds like a job for the wrist-watch scam."

"What's that?" I inquired.

"You need a watch, a little piece of paper, and incredibly tiny handwriting," he directed. "Write all the answers you need on that paper, and then attach it to the face of your watch. When you need an answer you just glance at your watch. The teacher will never guess you are cheating, just that you're nervous about how much time is left."

I was in the presence of a creative genius. And passing my German class looked much more promising.

The next Friday I was ready to implement the German-verb test strategy. The teacher told us to take out a piece of notebook paper and something to write with before putting everything else under our desks.

"Look straight ahead," she barked. "No copying off

anyone else's paper." I smiled to myself—of course, I had
no intention of copying off my neighbor's paper. When
she finished writing the German verbs on the board, I
attempted to be on the up and up. I immediately realized,
though, that none of these verbs were remotely tucked in
my memory. But . . . most of them were written on the face
of my watch.

So I began to flagrantly cheat. I did my best to make
my glances nonchalant, rather than staring at the lexicon
of wunderbar words.

Apparently, my acting ability was far from Oscar-
worthy. Three or four verbs into my quest for a passing
grade, the German teacher was just a few feet away from
me, making a beeline for my desk.

"Abort, abort," I whispered into my watch, not sure
who I was talking to. Then at that moment
I recalled Student Leader Cheater's emergency plan for such a crisis.

As subtle as an army tank at the Indy
500, I began to stretch and yawn. I covered
my mouth with my left hand and wrist to
"stifle" my yawn, my watch strategically
placed over my mouth. With a deft move,
I ate the paper. Polished off the verbs,
destroyed the evidence, sent conjugations
to the stomach.

> **As subtle as
> an army tank
> at the Indy 500,
> I began to
> stretch and
> yawn.**

But my moves didn't fool the teacher one bit. She obvi-
ously studied under Dr. Heimlich because before I knew

it she had pulled me out of my desk, positioned herself behind me, and proceeded to administer the maneuver.

I call it the Second Coming of My Conjugations.

The story ends with a fascinating conversation with the teacher and an assistant principal, multiple appearances at after-school meetings, and overall embarrassment on my part.

The moral of the story is: Kids, don't try this at home—or in class, for that matter. Cheating doesn't get you anywhere. In my case, not only do I know nothing about chemistry, but it also took me five years to get credit for two years of German.

No, I am no role model in this regard, other than to say I learned from my mistakes and now try to live as honestly as I can.

That's why I consider honesty number two on the Short List.

## THE SECOND IMPORTANT THING:
## Honesty

I've never been afraid of flying. I'm no gotta-take-a-train-or-a-bus kind of guy because I'm afraid the plane will crash. No, I believe the safest part of the trip is in the air. It's the nuts on the freeways who bother me.

But there is one nagging, silly little worry that I have about flying. I am always afraid that one day I am going to get on the wrong airplane!

I know there are computers at the gates designed to red-flag any boarding pass that doesn't match the correct destination. I also know there are competent airline personnel who ensure that a mistake of this nature is not going to happen. Nonetheless, it still scares me.

Case in point: I was sitting on an airplane ready to depart for Chicago when a gate agent's voice came over the plane's intercom. "Mr. Johnson? Mr. Bob Johnson? Can you ring your flight attendant call button, please?"

Mr. Johnson, who was seated a row behind me, pushed his call button. The gate agent strolled down the center aisle, leaned over to Mr. Johnson, and said, "This plane is not going to Omaha—it is going to Chicago. You'll need to grab your stuff and deplane right away!"

Well, maybe on some flight plan, Omaha is on the way to Chicago, or maybe Bob secretly wanted to go to Chicago instead of Omaha, but how did he get on our plane in the first place? Sometimes the bright human misses the dumb computer's error.

I can empathize with Bob Johnson because I'm anxious that it will happen to me.

A few years ago I was flying home to Orange County, California, from one of my out-of-town speaking engagements. I had flown to Chicago filled with energy, enthusiasm, vim, and vigor. Now I was returning home tired, worn-out, and (pardon the pun) on autopilot.

The plane landed in Orange County, and I deplaned as I do about a hundred times a year. I walked to the escalator that would take me to the baggage-claim level. I moved in almost a trancelike state, never thinking twice about anything. I plodded along, like I always do.

As the escalator descended, I suddenly awoke from my stupor when my eyes zeroed in on five large words.

Halfway down, as the lower level came into full view, I saw a large banner that said in bright red letters: WELCOME TO BOSTON LOGAN AIRPORT.

I couldn't believe it. *It's finally happened*, I said to myself. *I've gotten on the wrong plane, and no one caught the mistake.* I shuddered as I thought of the implications. Not only was I not in California, I was about as far away from home as one could be in the continental United States.

I shook my head in disbelief. It was while my head was wagging back and forth that reality came into focus.

On my left, over by the baggage carousels, was a jungle of cameras, lights, cables, and confusion . . .

they were making a movie at the airport!

Sure enough, I spotted Steve Martin and Goldie Hawn sitting in their movie-star chairs, while Mr. Martin's stunt double was being spit out of the belly of the baggage carousel.

Thank goodness I was really in Orange County, not Boston! Looking back, it's a pretty funny scene, but at the time I was pretty upset. I thought I had been deceived. Someone had been dishonest by telling me to get on a plane I thought was flying home when in fact it was flying as far from home as I could get.

Honesty is one of those virtues most of us just take for

> **My eyes zeroed in on five large words: WELCOME TO BOSTON LOGAN AIRPORT.**

granted. Some people may even be peeved that I would dare to suggest they are not always honest. No disrespect intended, but knowing life as I do, I think we can all use a little refresher course on honesty. I am making it the second most important character trait on the Short List. Let's take a look at its multiple facets.

### *An Honest Person Speaks the Truth to Himself or Herself*

Personal honesty is what we often refer to as integrity. It's what you and I are like when no one else is looking.

One of the best descriptions of personal integrity comes from the pen of King Solomon. He writes in the book of Proverbs:

> Guard your heart above all else,
> for it determines the course of your life.
> Avoid all perverse talk;
> stay away from corrupt speech.
> Look straight ahead,
> and fix your eyes on what lies before you.
> Mark out a straight path for your feet;
> stay on the safe path.
> Don't get sidetracked;
> keep your feet from following evil.
> PROVERBS 4:23-27

One of the things I find most interesting about this passage is the way it is constructed. In seminary, we were taught the importance of context—the best way to

understand a verse in the Bible is to first examine the verse
that precedes it and the verse that follows it. Often it is
through the context that we gain greater insight into a
verse's meaning.

I'll admit that this is an effective method of Bible
study that works in sixty-five out of the sixty-six books
of the Bible. But one book is the exception. You guessed
it—Proverbs. When Solomon and his boys put this book
together, it was more of a collection of wise sayings than a
book that found greater meaning through context. Some
passages are connected, but most are not. For example,
verse 6 in one chapter might talk about wise use of money,
while verse 7 might reflect on keeping your tongue in
check and verse 8 might instruct you on the best way to
treat a foolish person. The three ideas don't necessarily go
together.

So that is why I find this passage in Proverbs 4 so
intriguing. Unlike most places in the book, there is an
order here. The context is important in understanding
what being honest with yourself really looks like.

Solomon begins his short list of personal integrity traits
by *telling us to guard what we think.* First, he says, "Guard
your heart above all else" (v. 23). In biblical times, the heart
was thought of in the same way that our brain is today; in
other words, it was the seat of a person's thoughts and emotions. Solomon warns us: it all begins in the mind, so keep
it honest. When we get in trouble, it is usually because our

minds initiate an action that leads us into sin. In the New Testament, James describes it this way:

> Temptation comes from our own desires, which entice us and drag us away. These desires give birth to sinful actions. And when sin is allowed to grow, it gives birth to death.
> JAMES 1:14-15

> **In biblical times, the heart was considered the seat of a person's thoughts and emotions.**

The King James Version uses the word *lust* for *desires*, both of which have great power. Our evil thoughts lead to sin, and sin gives birth to death, which Scripture says is separation from God. So our evil thinking gets us in trouble and distances us from our heavenly Father. Not a good deal at all.

Honesty begins with a tough look at our thought lives. What occupies your mind when there is nothing else to think about? Do those sorts of thoughts honor God? Would you want your family to know you are thinking those things? Are you actually aware that those thoughts could manifest themselves into actions that would be hurtful, embarrassing, and shameful?

If your thought life is beyond your control, perhaps it is time to seek some help. Talk to your pastor, a trusted friend, or a competent counselor about the thoughts that plague you. In doing so, you will avoid years of potential heartache that could occur if you permit the thoughts to give way to actions.

Second, King Solomon takes hold of our tongues by *urging us to guard what we say.* "Avoid all perverse talk; stay away from corrupt speech" (v. 24). This seems to be a no-brainer for an honest person. If you're honest, you say only things that are true. *I do not lie*, you say to yourself. *I tell it like it is.* We'll get back to that later.

Third, King Solomon warns us *to guard what we see.* Personal honesty goes beyond pure thoughts and truthful words. It means to "look straight ahead, and fix your eyes on what lies before you" (v. 25). It's been a struggle for men and women of every generation, but it seems to be even harder in our world today. For all the benefits the Internet has given us, it is also a potential killer. It seems that everywhere I travel, I talk to both men and women who are addicted to the pornographic images that are so readily available online. What used to be found only in an adult magazine or XXX movie is a click away on the family laptop. For some people, the temptation is just too great. They have the self-control to avoid buying that magazine and would never slip into an exotic club, but the accessibility right there in the study is just too much to turn down.

For you, maybe the issue isn't on your computer, but in the way you look at other people, or the shows you watch on television, or the books and magazines you read. The point, says Solomon, is to look only at things that enhance your integrity, not those things that drag it down.

Job, the man in the Bible who suffered incredible losses in every aspect of his life, knew the importance of keeping his eyes focused on the right things. He said:

> I made a covenant with my eyes not to look with lust at a young woman.   JOB 31:1

That is good counsel for all of us, men or women, young or old. As the King James Version phrases Solomon's words in Proverbs 4:25, "Let thine eyes look right on"!

Fourth, Solomon tells us *to guard where we walk.* Honesty in your personal life and mine is captured in these words: "Mark out a straight path for your feet; stay on the safe path" (Proverbs 4:26).

Pretty simple? Well, not exactly. The "list" of acceptable and unacceptable places differs among Christian brothers and sisters.

"I travel constantly for business," my friend said as he began our conversation over a cup of coffee. "I am always entertaining clients and prospective clients. So I know the advantage of giving clients a dining experience not soon to be forgotten."

"Sounds good to me," I said.

"Yeah. So far, so good," he replied. "But the problem for me is that lots of these clients want to hit the local bar for a nightcap after the dinner. I know plenty of good

Christian folks who wouldn't mind accompanying their clients to their late-night meetings because they exercise plenty of self-control. It's no big deal."

"Go on," I prodded.

"But for me going into a bar *is* a big deal," my friend confessed. "I come from a family of alcoholics, and I'm not all that strong when it comes to self-control. In other words, for me, entering a bar is a disaster waiting to happen."

"Will your boss fire you for not accompanying your clients to the bar?" I asked.

"No," my friend answered.

"Can you make the sale with your prospective clients without joining them in the bar?" I continued.

"Sure—I do it all the time!" he exclaimed.

"Well then, stay out of the bar," I replied.

"Really?" he asked.

"If bars are places you shouldn't be, then I'd make it a priority to stay out of them—at all costs."

> "Do life righteously," Solomon advises.

We're not talking about rocket science, folks. We're talking about godliness, integrity, and personal honesty. Like my friend, you can make the right decision about where you walk.

Finally, in Proverbs 4:27, Solomon implores us *to guard what we do*: "Don't get sidetracked; keep your feet from following evil." In many ways, this last admonition is the most all-encompassing of them all.

Essentially, he's saying, "Do life righteously." In every area, not just select portions. Make it true; apply it to the whole megillah.

If you're wondering, *Where am I going to get the strength to fight these areas in which I struggle?* keep reading—there will be an answer before this chapter ends.

For now, recognize once we have personal honesty in place, we are ready to move on to honesty in relationships.

### An Honest Person Speaks the Truth to Others

Can you remember your parents or maybe your teacher using the illustration of George Washington chopping down the cherry tree as an example of an honest person? When confronted with the deed (so the story goes), the young Washington did not hide his guilt. "I cannot tell a lie, Father. I did it." It was a statement that inspired millions of us as youngsters. To this day, it is hard for me to read the historians who claim that the cherry tree story never happened. Somehow, it just doesn't seem honest.

But there is no controversy in the Scriptures when it comes to being honest with each other. Pleas for honesty are sprinkled throughout the Bible, with many of these statements uttered by King Solomon, the apostle Paul, and of course, Jesus Himself.

To my way of thinking, the best and most concise statement on being honest with others comes from Paul:

> Instead, we will speak the truth in love, growing in every
> way more and more like Christ, who is the head of his body,
> the church.   EPHESIANS 4:15

I love the succinctness of the phrase "speak the truth in love." Not only does it command us to be honest, but it also guides us on how to make that honesty more effectively accepted by the listener. Let's break down the phrase even more.

First, Paul gets right to the point: speak the truth and nothing but the truth. He is pleading for honesty, pure and simple. There is never a good reason to lie. There is never a good reason to tell a little white lie. There is never a good reason to "bend the truth just a little." No, Paul says in no uncertain terms, always speak the truth. When I was a child, I sometimes resorted to fudging the truth. It was mostly the truth but not entirely the truth. Fudging is not acceptable in Paul's book.

Second, Paul completes the phrase with two added key words: speak the truth *in love*. Ah, the love component. Not everyone needs to be reminded to speak the truth with love, but people who bark the truth harshly with a side of arrogance definitely need it. It's the "I call 'em as I see 'em" person who, though honest, has a gruff and edgy personality that makes the truth harder to accept.

Psychologists have known for a long time that this distinction is one of the ways you can divide the population: half of us tend to tell the truth no matter whom it hurts, while the other half tend to water down the truth, taking into account the other person's feelings. In the Myers-Briggs Type Indicator, for example, the former group is known as Thinkers and the latter group is known as Feelers.

> **Half of us tend to tell the truth no matter whom it hurts, while the other half tend to take into account the other person's feelings.**

Thinkers speak their minds. They love to offer criticism because, to them, criticism makes things better. They also receive criticism well because they are open to critiques that reflect the truth.

Feelers, on the other hand, don't necessarily lie, but they frame the truth in more loving terms. They rarely hand out criticism to another person, and they find it extremely difficult to be critiqued by others.

To give you a mental image, some of us are rough and fearsome Attila the Huns while the rest of us are big purple Barneys.

The question is: how can truth tellers be more loving, and how can lovers be more truthful? The wisest man who ever lived has the answer: speak the truth in love with tact. Solomon put it this way:

> Everyone enjoys a fitting reply;
>> it is wonderful to say the right thing at the right time!
> PROVERBS 15:23

What is it about a fitting reply that people find so engaging, that makes them respond more positively? A

fitting reply means that I am exercising more care as I prepare what I am going to say, that I am choosing words that
are the best and said at the right time, without compromis-
ing the truthfulness of the statement made.

Certainly this is a worthy goal, but how can you and
I be tactful and truthful on a regular basis? Again, we
consult Proverbs:

> The heart of the godly thinks carefully before speaking;
>     the mouth of the wicked overflows with evil words.
>     PROVERBS 15:28

A godly person thinks carefully before speaking.
"Think before you speak" is not just a trite expression your
mother used to drum into you—usually after you didn't.
It's good, godly counsel. One of my mentors used to say
that the root word in Hebrew for *think* in that verse could
be translated *hmmmm*. I am not certain that his translation was verbatim from the Hebrew, but what a brilliant
concept. When it's your turn to respond to someone in a
difficult situation, stop before you open your mouth, and
say *hmmmm* to yourself—just long enough to formulate an
answer that is truthful, loving, and tactful.

Carefully consider Solomon's words:

> There is more hope for a fool
>     than for someone who speaks without thinking.
>     PROVERBS 29:20

Tact really is a key concept. With tact, Attila the Hun becomes more loving without sacrificing the truth. And Barney becomes more truthful without hurting the person being addressed.

We've looked at being honest with ourselves and honest with other people, but I've saved the most important person to be honest with for last.

### An Honest Person Speaks the Truth to God

Consider it as dominoes falling in reverse. We're not going to be completely honest with other people until we are honest with ourselves. And we are not going be totally honest with ourselves until we determine to be honest with God.

> Responding to someone in a difficult situation? Say *hmmmm* to yourself—long enough to formulate an answer that is truthful, loving, and tactful.

To anyone who counters, "Oh, I can be honest with myself without dealing with God," I would suggest that not dealing with God is not being honest with Him. It's like saying you're completely committed to running a marathon and then fooling everyone by sneaking into the pack halfway through the race (it certainly has been done!) and heading to the finish line. To truly claim that you ran a marathon, you must start at the beginning and do your best to finish as many miles as you can to honor your commitment completely. In the same way, you must become honest with God in order to be totally honest in your life.

Here's the best news of all: being honest with God is the most wonderful thing you could do in your life! It doesn't mean you'll be serving a prison sentence or leaving all your fun behind. Rather, it's meeting someone who can personally change your life.

Jesus has been liberating folks for centuries. The apostle John overheard a conversation Jesus had with some of His followers about this very issue. Here's how John saw it:

> **You must become honest with God in order to be totally honest in your life.**

> Jesus said to the people who believed in him, "You are truly my disciples if you remain faithful to my teachings. And you will know the truth, and the truth will set you free."
>
> "But we are descendants of Abraham," they said. "We have never been slaves to anyone. What do you mean, 'You will be set free'?"
>
> Jesus replied, "I tell you the truth, everyone who sins is a slave of sin. A slave is not a permanent member of the family, but a son is part of the family forever. So if the Son sets you free, you are truly free." JOHN 8:31-36

Three things make up the heart of Jesus' teachings. *First, the truth is in His Word.* In John's Gospel, Jesus says, "Remain faithful to my teachings." Early in the first century, people had the advantage of sitting in a crowd on a hillside and hearing Jesus teach publicly or even having a one-to-one conversation with Him. I must admit that sometimes I am envious of people who had that privilege.

So what about those of us in the twenty-first century? We can't hear Jesus preaching in a stadium or see Larry King asking Jesus questions about His teachings. How do we interact with His teachings? Through His Word, the Bible. God has left us with more than what some people consider an inspired collection of sayings. In the Bible, God is literally speaking to us. Jesus invites us to be part of something specific. Not a religion or a set of rules, but a personal relationship. Not only is Jesus the Savior of the world, He invites us to accept Him as our personal Savior.

What happens when we accept this truth? *The truth sets us free.* In John 8:32, Jesus says to His disciples, "And you will know the truth, and the truth will set you free." I am amazed at how many people are shocked to hear that Jesus was the one who first spoke those words. The promise of freedom is used throughout our culture to tout everything from politics to sleeping pills. What I love so much about those words from Jesus is that they ring with grace, not guilt or shame.

Okay, the truth sets us free—but free from what? That's exactly what some of Jesus' followers asked Him. "We have never been slaves to anyone," they respond. So what do they need to be freed from?

Sin. Jesus was talking about being a slave to sin. In the first part of this chapter, we explored what area in your life is the biggest struggle for you: what you think, what you say, what you see, where you walk, or what you do. What robs you of your joy? What grabs you by the throat and won't let you go? It's that secret sin, that obsession, that addiction, that hidden indiscretion.

That is precisely why Jesus came to earth—to free you from that sin. *You don't have to be a slave to that sin because Jesus' truth offers you the power to overcome it.* It doesn't matter how long you have struggled with it without victory. It doesn't matter how perverse it may seem to you or others. The point is Jesus came to nail that sin to the Cross so it wouldn't nail you into submission.

It's possible because of God's agape love. It's a supernatural power. Just as God's love can permeate you, God can also pour His truth into you so that you can be freed from the chains of your sinful past. That's something only God can do.

Solomon said it well:

> Evil people are trapped by sin,
> but the righteous escape, shouting for joy.
> PROVERBS 29:6

Jesus tells His followers in this passage that *trusting His Truth brings a freedom unlike any other.* "If the Son sets you free, you are truly free" (John 8:36). What Jesus offers is so beyond what anyone else can offer, it defies comparison. Anyone, including me, would be a fool to pass up the offer of an eternal connection with the God of the universe. It's the truth that sets us free.

If I am going to commit myself to honesty—number two on the Short List—I have to let the love of God flow through me—even to the unlovable people in my life. I need to see the Lord Jesus face-to-face and commit to knowing Him as the God of Truth, Truth personified.

It works.

Honest.

# CHAPTER THREE

# The Lesson from Big Buttermobile

My five children, Joy, Jesse, Jeffrey, John, and Joseph, are all grown-up, moved out, and living life as fully functioning adults. Joy, Jesse, and Jeffrey are married with children of their own. There's nothing like grandchildren to help you relive the events that shaped your life when their parents were the same age. In my mind's eye, I can see my daughter, Joy, in her daughters, Jill and Jenna; my son Jesse in his sons, Liam and Finn; and my son Jeffrey in his daughters, Ava and Ellie. The fact that they are so much alike is simultaneously charming, quaint, and definitely a little scary.

Some things never change from one generation to the next. There are still pacifiers, favorite baby blankets, and footie pajamas to go along with the immutable rules of nature—the aroma of a dirty diaper needing adult intervention, the comfort baby feels from sucking his or her thumb, and the crankiness that comes with cutting teeth.

But other things have changed. Necessities such as high chairs, car seats, cribs, and playpens have become more technologically advanced. Back in my new-to-fathering days, little ones could lounge in an "infant seat." It was a baby-sized piece of molded plastic shaped to cradle a baby, complete with a movable handle that propped up the infant seat when you weren't carrying Junior from room to room. My wife or I would carry the baby out to the car in the infant seat and then transfer the child from the infant seat to the car seat in one continuous scoop and swoop. Nowadays, my youngest grandkids' infant seats are actually a removable part of their car seats, eliminating the need for the transfer from one seat to the other.

You've come a long way, baby.

And speaking of technological advances, let's not forget the automobiles that transport those car seats. Medium-sized cars gave birth to larger cars that led to the classic station wagons that gave way to passenger vans that spawned the "tricked out" customized vans that downsized to minivans that currently have been eclipsed by today's family SUVs (which may soon be replaced by the family armada of scooters if the price of gas keeps going up).

My kids' vehicles are like homes away from home—complete with individual heating and cooling systems, state-of-the-art CD sound systems, and my personal favorite, DVD players with personal screens and headphones. Traveling with those kinds of accoutrements is something I could only dream about on a first-class airplane ticket.

All six of my grandchildren are currently under the age of six. Seeing them in this home theater on wheels, I am convinced that Disney is behind the bells and whistles of cars today. Almost every CD and DVD in those minivans and SUVs has Walt's signature on it somewhere. No long-term Mickey Mouse strategic faux pas for that guy, if you ask me.

Cool cars aside, nothing can erase from my memory the scene of unbridled enthusiasm from my kids when I drove home from the used car lot with our first full-size family vehicle . . . our Pontiac station wagon. Since they had been cooped up in subcompact cars their entire lives, this was a big moment!

The station wagon is a mode of transportation from which legends are made. It's been fascinating to see cars expand and shrink over the years. I believe I've owned one of every dimension. But of course when I daydream about the quintessential family station wagon, I always see our "Big Buttermobile," as we fondly nicknamed it. (Years later we would graduate to the full-size van, which we named Butterbus.) Any station wagon worthy of being called a station wagon

**The station wagon is a mode of transportation from which legends are made.**

had wood paneling on the sides. Rumor has it that original "woodies" actually had real wood adorning the sides, but by the time I could afford a station wagon, the wood paneling was top-of-the-line, handcrafted, wood-grain contact paper. Our vehicle wasn't called Big Buttermobile for nothing. Just envision an aircraft carrier with wood-grain contact paper on each side—that's a station wagon from the sixties or seventies!

So when our fourth child, John, was born, the big boat with the optional third row of seats was perfect for us, just like the salesman at Cal Worthington's used car lot told us it would be. Dad and Mom sat up front, the two youngest kids were in their car seats in the middle row, and the two oldest kids were all the way in the back on that wonderful backseat that faced the scenery behind us. I believe this seat was placed that way to ensure headaches, dizziness, and nausea. Kids *loved* it. Sure, Big Buttermobile guzzled gas, but gas was cheaper and there were no shortages to worry about back then. It was the good old days: pumping leaded gasoline, ingesting all kinds of trans fats out of Styrofoam containers, and littering freely. Actually, I did try to be somewhat responsible. I drove a little compact car around town when the entire family didn't need to be transported.

One issue that was a bane for our young family was regularly attending church. When Sunday rolled around, the spirit was willing but the flesh was weak. Almost every Sunday one of our children had some sort of communicable disease that made going to church a medical impossibility. "Joy has the sniffles, so I can't take her to her class," my wife would lament one week. Or Jesse had a fever. Or Jeffrey had a cough. Or Johnny had a runny nose.

So rather than risk a personal escort from church by someone from the Centers for Disease Control, the patient and one parent would stay home from the Sunday service. Until I came up with a brilliant idea.

That's right. I figured out a way for every family member (except the ailing child) to attend church every Sunday. You need two adults, two cars, and a church that offers at least two identical morning services.

Here's the way it works. One parent loads the car with some healthy kids for the first worship service. As the early service is ending, the second parent arrives with the second group of healthy kids and the sick kid. In the church parking lot, you smoothly accomplish a Chinese fire drill–like maneuver with the first shift greeting the second shift before changing places; the sick child never moves in this scenario. Voilá! Except for the child with the ailment of the week, everyone gets to church and the rest of the churchgoing population is not exposed to a communicable disease.

A truly masterful plan . . .

for the one and only time we tried it.

It was Saturday evening, and John, our youngest at the time, was still an infant. This particular weekend he was sick and in no condition to be taken to church. "I'll go to the early service," I volunteered, "and I'll take any child who is well and ready to go at 8:20 a.m.!"

My wife smiled weakly. She must have had inside information on how this drama would unfold.

Bright and early the next morning, I began my morning routine: drink coffee, shower, shave, get dressed, and spend a little quiet time to journal and get my head together for the day.

"It's 8:20!" I announced. "Who's ready to go to church with Daddy?"

To my astonishment (and mine alone), absolutely no one was ready to go. My wife gave me a look that translated, *Did you really think preschoolers were going to get ready all by themselves?* Oh yes, I forgot that part.

"Well, I guess I'll have to go alone," I ventured meekly. "I'll take the little car and meet you in the church parking lot at 10:40 to make the swap. Then I'll bring little Johnny home with me."

My wife still gave me that weak smile, so I decided to get out while I still had a chance.

The worship service that morning was wonderful. The music was heavenly. The message was meaningful. I vowed to love God and hate the devil all the rest of my days as I bounded out at the conclusion of the service and headed straight for the parking lot.

There it was—Big Buttermobile making the turn and heading my way. *Everything's going according to the plan,*

I thought, deeply entrenched in how ingenious my idea really was.

As the station wagon got closer, I saw my wife's face; her look was off the stress charts. Her fingers were clenching the steering wheel so hard that her white knuckles glistened in the sunlight.

I guessed she wasn't having a good morning.

Maybe the Bible on the roof of the car was news that I should have left alone.

But I was impressed. She had driven all the way across town with her Bible on the top of the station wagon. She must have placed it there before buckling one of the kids into his car seat. As she stopped the car next to me, I shouted, "Your Bible is on the roof of the car!"

To her, it must have felt as if I were beckoning fellow churchgoers like a barker at a sideshow. "Look everyone. My wife's Bible is on the roof of the car!"

"Get in the car," my wife muttered as the kids piled out of the vehicle.

"Your Bible's on the roof of the car!" I felt like a cheerleader.

"Get in the car, Bill," she said, her already stressed-out voice growing in intensity.

"Hey." I changed tactics. "Your Bible is open to the book of Job. How appropriate!"

> **I was impressed. My wife had driven all the way across town with her Bible on the top of the station wagon.**

It was at that moment that my wife pulled me into the car through the side vent.

"What's the matter?" I asked, still clueless. "Your Bible safely made it all the way to church."

*"My* purse *was on the roof of the car, too, you doofus!"*

With that pronouncement, we all jumped into the station wagon and retraced our route in reverse. (The route was in reverse, not the station wagon.) Hopefully, the purse would be unscathed on the side of the road somewhere between church and home.

Putt, putt, putting along at two miles per hour for thorough-scouring purposes, we finally made it home, where said missing purse was lying right next to our driveway!

Apparently when my wife brought John out to put him in the car seat, she placed the Bible and her purse on the car roof while she buckled him in. She intended to grab them after he was settled in, but with all the commotion of packing up the kids, somehow it escaped her memory.

That story is part of our family history, one I have told hundreds of times. Do you know what happens when I tell that story at one of my presentations? People will come up afterward and share their own personal roof-of-the-car stories.

I've heard of books on the roof of the car. I've heard of doctoral dissertations on the roof of the car. I've heard of coffee mugs with fresh brew on the roof of the car. I've heard of infant seats on the roof of the car. And believe it or not, I've even heard of infant seats with the infants still in them on the roof of the car. (I've got the newspaper article to prove it.)

Yes, everybody has his or her own version of a roof-of-the-car story, and for Christians, everybody has a story about faith.

How they believed that God loved them personally, how they depended on God to get them into medical school, how they trusted God to find them a spouse, how they had the faith to launch a new endeavor, and how faith—along the way—helped them through the tough times.

The fact that stories of faith are written every day takes nothing away from their power. If anything, it strengthens them, because it's something that connects us to each other.

That's why I think faith deserves a spot on the Short List.

THE THIRD IMPORTANT THING:

## Faith

The first two important things in life are love and honesty.
The Lord Jesus emphasized the importance of both qualities, so it makes sense that they would make the Short List.

But where do we go from there?

Thinking back to 1 Corinthians 13:13, which we
looked at on page 18, Paul talks about love as the supreme
character quality. But he includes two other characteristics:
faith and hope.

I first professed my personal faith in the Lord Jesus
more than fifty years ago. I have had periods in my life of
deep, intense faith, and I have had times that Jesus might
refer to as times of "little faith." During my times of strong
faith, I realize how interconnected faith and hope can

be. In this chapter we want to unwrap another passage of Scripture that speaks specifically about faith—our ability to trust in the Lord, no matter what is happening in our lives.

I can trust God completely (faith) because of the certainty I have in Him (hope). It is a bit like a two-for-one deal!

What does it really mean to be a person of faith? What does a faithful person look like? On page 16, we looked at Paul's first letter to the church at Thessalonica. I love this letter to them because Paul is cheering them on to continue doing the right things. Not only does Paul mention the crucial role of love in that letter, he mentions how faith plays a major role too. We can see at least three ways Paul identifies people who are faithful.

### *A Faithful Person Believes the Right Stuff*
Early in the book of 1 Thessalonians, Paul congratulates the believers, not only for their faith, but more significantly for placing their faith in the right source—God and the power of His Holy Spirit. Here's what Paul says:

> As we pray to our God and Father about you, we think of your faithful work, your loving deeds, and the enduring hope you have because of our Lord Jesus Christ. . . .
>
> For when we brought you the Good News, it was not only with words but also with power, for the Holy Spirit gave you full assurance that what we said was true. And you know of our concern for you from the way we lived when we were with you. . . .

> Therefore, we never stop thanking God that when you
> received his message from us, you didn't think of our words
> as mere human ideas. You accepted what we said as the very
> word of God—which, of course, it is. And this word continues
> to work in you who believe.   1 THESSALONIANS 1:3, 5; 2:13

Did you notice? Paul begins by thanking God for the Thessalonians' *faithful* work. That's true biblical faith, faith in action. "I am grateful," Paul essentially says, "that even after I left you, the faith you began while I was with you not only has remained, but it is growing." Paul reminds me of a parent, writing to a son or daughter at college, expressing gratitude that his child has remained firm in his or her Christian beliefs and has not run off and joined some crazy cult. He is a proud dad.

What makes him proud of the Thessalonians' faith? The key is the person whom they placed their faith in. The word *faith* is overused in our culture today. An athlete hits the winning home run because he had faith. A politician edges out her opponent because she has faith. A guy wins the lottery because he has faith. *Faith* seems to be the word of choice in our world. Sometimes it sounds like what is really being said is "I have faith in faith."

Just having faith is not enough. In order for faith to be faith, you must have faith in something—a person or a teaching. As Christians, we place our faith in the true living Savior of the world, the Lord Jesus, because we trust that He is who He says He is.

Believing in Jesus is believing the right stuff. He is the object of our faith. And He is powerful. Paul says that when he brought the Thessalonians the gospel message, it was not just with words but with power. He had been given authority to speak on God's behalf. Paul was not voicing his human thoughts. He was delivering the power of God to his listeners.

> **Believing in Jesus is believing the right stuff. He is the object of our faith.**

My favorite use of the word *power* in Paul's writings can be found in his letter to the Romans:

> For I am not ashamed of this Good News about Christ. It is the power of God at work, saving everyone who believes—the Jew first and also the Gentile.   ROMANS 1:16

The English spelling for the Greek word translated "power" is *dunamis*. It's the word from which we get our English word *dynamite*. I love that etymological connection—we can say that God's power is like a keg of dynamite. Growing up watching TV Westerns, I always looked forward to episodes where the old prospector would blow up the mine—with the bad guys inside—with a bundle of dynamite sticks. To this day, it's still a mystery to me how a small object that looks like a cross between a hot dog and a candle can pack such explosive power.

Remember how we looked at having the *power* to love people who are unlovable? Remember how we examined having the *power* to defeat the struggles that enslave us? That's God's power, the power that comes to us from tapping into the Good News of the gospel.

How do you get that kind of power? Well, as a child I thought I had to work for it. "Good boys go to heaven and bad boys go to hell" was a theology I learned somewhere in early life. It was when I was in high school that I discovered I wasn't the only person to misunderstand how the concept of "works" plays into our relationship with God.

When Jesus walked the earth, there were people who were confused about the same issue. Here's a snippet of the conversation that took place between Jesus and some of His followers:

> They replied, "We want to perform God's works, too. What should we do?"
>
> Jesus told them, "This is the only work God wants from you: Believe in the one he has sent." JOHN 6:28-29

Essentially, they were saying, "We want to do good works to get in good with God. So tell us what good works will benefit us most!"

Jesus answers with the only "work" that we can do— believe in Him. Trust Him. Depend upon Him. Have faith in Him. It's all the same thing.

Years later, Paul would write:

God saved you by his grace when you believed. And you can't take credit for this; it is a gift from God. Salvation is not a reward for the good things we have done, so none of us can boast about it.   EPHESIANS 2:8-9

If you've never understood that a relationship with God is not based on works but on faith, why not take a minute and place your own personal faith in the Lord Jesus? When I finally understood the Good News, I said a prayer that went something like this:

> *Lord, there are so many things I don't understand, but I now realize that You died on the cross for all I've done wrong and offer me Your forgiveness. So right now, the best I know how, I receive You as my personal Savior. Thank You for giving me a relationship with You and eternal life as a free gift.*

The Bible says that as soon as I prayed that prayer, I was born into the family of God. I am His child. And when I die, I will go to be with Him in heaven for all eternity. (Check out verses like John 3:16; John 6:47; Acts 16:31; and 1 John 5:13.) I'd be a fool to pass up an offer like that. See, it's not just faith—it's faith in Jesus.

Not only do we see that faith's object—Jesus Christ—is powerful, we also see that faith's object is supernatural. In 1 Thessalonians 2:13, Paul says, "You accepted what we said as the very word of God—which, of course, it is. And this word continues to work in you who believe." Paul explains why his words can have such power—they are coming from God Himself!

The powerful nature of our faith is directly connected to the supernatural nature of our faith. Because we are doing more than exercising faith—anyone can do that— by exercising faith in Christ, the object of our faith taps us into power beyond our wildest imaginations.

But there's a second way Paul says we can recognize a faithful person.

### A Faithful Person Makes the Necessary Changes

Paul definitely gives high scores to the believers in Thessalonica. Word has gotten around about what they've been doing. As the book begins, Paul commends them on how they have put their faith to work.

> And now the word of the Lord is ringing out from you to people everywhere, even beyond Macedonia and Achaia, for wherever we go we find people telling us about your faith in God. We don't need to tell them about it, for they keep talking about the wonderful welcome you gave us and how you turned away from idols to serve the living and true God. 1 THESSALONIANS 1:8-9

How was their faith demonstrated? By the way they "turned away from idols to serve the living and true God."

It doesn't matter what time in history you live in or what culture you grew up in: authentic Christian faith can be recognized by the change it produces in our lives. Jesus refers to it as the "fruit" that we bear.

> **Authentic Christian faith can be recognized by the change it produces in our lives.**

For the Thessalonian believers in Macedonia, idol worship was a regular part of their culture. In order to show people around them that they trusted in someone more powerful than idols, they needed to take action. They needed to consciously decide to stop worshiping these false gods.

Fast-forward to today. How does that apply to you and me? First of all, changing how we live pleases God. Paul states it clearly in the fourth chapter:

Finally, dear brothers and sisters, we urge you in the name of the Lord Jesus to live in a way that pleases God, as we have taught you. You live this way already, and we encourage you to do so even more. For you remember what we taught you by the authority of the Lord Jesus.    1 THESSALONIANS 4:1-2

Paul is commending these Gentile believers for turning away from idols, and he wants them to keep up the good work because it pleases God. Do you see the connection between our faith, our relationship with God, and our willingness to make necessary changes in our lives?

The desire to change can be motivated by many

things, but by far, the most excellent motivation is love. And as I've been writing this book, I've found it exciting to see how all of my Short List character qualities interrelate. My love is stronger because of my faith. My faith gains muscle because of my love. My honesty becomes easier because of my faith.

On a personal level, I know for a fact that there are changes in my life I never would have made had love not entered my world in the person of my wife, Kathi. She can ask me to do things I would never consider doing otherwise, but because the request is coming from her and I love her, I am willing to do them.

> **You can't say things have changed if they aren't any different.**

Faithful people make the necessary changes, and those changes please God. You can't say things have changed if they aren't any different.

Call it a matter of semantics, but people seem much more comfortable with the word *change* than they are with the word *different*. Both words can mean the same thing, but *change* often denotes a positive spin: growth, progress, and achievement. The word *different* can imply growth, progress, and achievement, but it also emphasizes the fact that you will not be the same after the change takes place.

In Scripture, that concept of "difference" embodies the word *holiness*. Paul puts it in context for the Thessalonian believers:

> God has called us to live holy [different] lives, not impure
> lives. Therefore, anyone who refuses to live by these rules
> is not disobeying human teaching but is rejecting God, who
> gives his Holy Spirit to you.    1 THESSALONIANS 4:7-8

The Greek word for *holiness* is *hagios*, meaning "set apart." But it also means *different*. It's not always a welcome idea, especially to newer Christians. "I can handle holiness," a friend once told me. "It's the 'different' part of the equation that really throws me a curve."

We need to be committed to the necessary changes that our faith requires. We also need to recognize that the goal is to make those changes permanent, not just temporary. The kinds of changes God wants are like permanent tattoos, not temporary ones. Little kids squeal with delight over temporary tattoos of their favorite cartoon characters on their arms; Mom and Dad are grateful that tomorrow's bath will wash away the evidence. But we've all heard the tattoo parlor "oops" stories where some guy has to explain to his beloved why he couldn't remember how to spell her name.

Just as tattoos are meant to be permanent, changes in our lives that reflect a spiritual change should be too. So many of us make changes, even holy ones, on a regular basis, but they fall by the wayside in a few short weeks. They're almost like religious "fads." Just as mood rings, pet rocks, and troll dolls were really big deals for a while before eventually fading into oblivion, we sometimes try to pick up a new spiritual habit, only to drop it within a few weeks or months. We need to get past what is "in" spiritually and construct a faith that produces a permanent change.

Paul identifies one more characteristic of a faithful person.

### A Faithful Person Is Not Immune from Pain

I don't know where the idea started, but regrettably some Christians believe that if you are a person of faith, you will never hurt again in any way, shape, or form. All I can say is that these folks must live in some sort of spiritual denial, because it simply is not true. Paul made this quite clear to the Thessalonian believers.

> Finally, when we could stand it no longer, we decided to stay alone in Athens, and we sent Timothy to visit you. He is our brother and God's co-worker in proclaiming the Good News of Christ. We sent him to strengthen you, to encourage you in your faith, and to keep you from being shaken by the troubles you were going through. But you know that we are destined for such troubles. Even while we were with you, we warned you that troubles would soon come—and they did, as you well know. That is why, when I could bear it no longer, I sent Timothy to find out whether your faith was still strong. I was afraid that the tempter had gotten the best of you and that our work had been useless.
>
> But now Timothy has just returned, bringing us good news about your faith and love. He reports that you always

remember our visit with joy and that you want to see us as much as we want to see you. So we have been greatly encouraged in the midst of our troubles and suffering, dear brothers and sisters, because you have remained strong in your faith. It gives us new life to know that you are standing firm in the Lord.   1 THESSALONIANS 3:1-8

One of the reasons Paul sent Timothy back to visit the Thessalonians was to keep them "from being shaken by the troubles [they] were going through" (v. 3). Pain is easily misunderstood. The Bible clearly teaches that Christians will go through painful circumstances. Not only is suffering painful, but it can also weaken our faith. The word translated *shaken* in verse 3 is also translated *disturbed* in other translations. The literal meaning of the Greek word refers to a dog wagging its tail; part of the intensity of pain is how it can make us vacillate in our faith.

> **Part of the intensity of pain is how it can make us vacillate in our faith.**

But one of the reasons faith made the Short List is because we all deal with pain in our lives and pain is put into perspective through our faith. "Even while we were with you, we warned you that troubles would soon come—and they did, as you well know" (v. 4) is Paul's way of saying what Peter reveals in his first letter: "Don't be surprised when life has trials." Bad things will happen to good people. Sometimes suffering is the result of our actions, as when a parent disciplines his or her child. But many times suffering is simply unexplainable.

Maybe Paul gives us a clue in another passage:

> Everyone who wants to live a godly life in Christ Jesus will suffer persecution.    2 TIMOTHY 3:12

If I am reading this verse correctly, it says that Christians will indeed suffer. But it goes further than that: Christians who suffer the most are the ones who are most deeply committed to godliness! How can that be? Because God uses pain in our lives to deepen our faith. We are stronger, deeper, better people because of some of the hardships we have been asked to endure.

I mentioned that I have possessed faith in the Savior for over fifty years. But I will admit that some years have been stronger than others. Without question, the seasons of the most profound depth in my faith were the seasons of suffering. Someone said pain either draws you closer to God or drives you further away. I'm thankful that, in my case, it has always been a magnet, drawing me closer to my Lord.

Sometimes it takes everything else in our world being stripped away from us before we realize how important God is in our lives. A few years ago, I reread twenty-five years worth of journaling. I relived everything from the high points of the births of each of my children through several of their weddings, to the low point of dealing with my divorce. I saw with fresh eyes how life's experiences never can be plotted as a straight line—there are myriad ups and downs. It was helpful to see the key concepts that I seemed to fall back on over and over again. If I were to condense my life into one phrase it would be:

*Only God won't disappoint.*

It was true in my life twenty years ago, and it's still true today. It was true for the believers at the church in Thessalonica, and it's true for the megachurch pastor today. It comforted Martin Luther just as it comforted Mother Teresa. It transcends time and economy, bringing comfort to princes and paupers.

Why?

Because its truth is rooted in our faith. No matter how difficult our circumstances, God simply asks us to trust Him. It is our faith that makes sense of the things we so easily misunderstand. It is our faith that makes suffering tolerable because the object of our faith is the Savior who suffered on our behalf to eradicate all the sin in the world. It is our faith that makes us different because it is our faith that makes all the difference in the world.

Faith definitely deserves to make the Short List. It belongs there. Trust me.

Better yet, trust Him.

# CHAPTER FOUR

# The Lesson from Cruising with the Doctor

I graduated from Dallas Theological Seminary with a master's degree. Actually, I received more than that as any DTS graduate can attest. You leave the hallowed halls with two long-term aftereffects:

- The desire to be a lifelong, die-hard Dallas Cowboys fan
- The ability to be conversant in "small-town Texas" stories, no matter where you hail from

For someone born and raised in Philadelphia and a die-hard Eagles fan, the first aftereffect certainly was a challenge. Changing team loyalties would be considered heretical. "God wants you to be a Cowboys fan" was never explicitly uttered, but it was regularly implied. With head coach Tom Landry on the board of the seminary, cheering for the silver and blue was up there with reading your Bible, praying, and parsing Greek verbs. Besides, Dallas Cowboys fans went to heaven, whereas Philadelphia Eagles fans went to Veterans Stadium, often for an exercise in frustration that felt like eternal separation from the living God.

Football aside, the second aftereffect was equally as fascinating. I was a big city and suburban guy; a small Texan town was as foreign to me as the daily prayers on behalf of Cowboys quarterback Roger Staubach. The seminary had students from all over the world, but the guys from these small Texan towns seemed legion. And for the most part, they were real characters.

My favorite guy of all was Bud. He wasn't just from Texas; Bud grew up in west Texas, which, according to him, made all the difference in the world. "Y'all know what I mean, y'all?" he would begin in his hypnotic Texas drawl. His words left his mouth in slow motion; today we would swear they had been digitally altered. But what he said sure stuck. I can still remember his descriptions:

- In east Texas they have big cities. Ain't none in west Texas.
- They got highways in east Texas. Ain't none in west Texas.
- East Texas got itself lots of people, lots of hills, lots of stuff. West Texas is just flat, lonely, and ugly.

I loved to listen to Bud tell his tales and spin his yarns, making me laugh with his fabrications. It wouldn't take much investigation to unravel his stories. Were there big cities and highways in west Texas? Of course. And, good night, everyone knows that all of Texas is flat.

No, with Bud it wasn't about checking out his sources or researching his references; it was all about telling the story. He was like Garrison Keillor with a slower delivery and a trademark twang.

Bud told a ton of tales, but in the midst of all the verbiage, it was easy to identify the stories that were true. There was a ring of authenticity in Bud's drawl and a change in his decorum that said he wasn't making this one up.

I recall the saga of Bud's quest for the Guinness World Record for shooting Dr. Pepper cans nonstop off a fence post. (According to Bud, "the Doctor" is the drink of choice in west Texas.) And I can almost imitate Bud imitating his mama's constant chide to "stop sittin' around and bein' so lazy—go out and shoot us some rattlesnake for supper!"

But the quintessential Bud story is a universal one for any high school kid: how can I get in good with the "cool" kids and join their ranks? It's a little tale about coming of age in west Texas.

If you wanted to be cool in Bud's town, you had to go cruising.

I'm certain that Henry Ford went cruising in his Model T on the streets of Detroit to impress the girls.

Some cruising is innocent; some cruising is a little more racy, but the common ingredients are

- young people (usually all of the same gender) crammed into a vehicle, the flashier the better
- driving less than 20 mph on the main drag in town
- all to get the attention of members of the opposite sex

In Bud's high school, there was an added ingredient to cruising: underage drinking. Bud didn't condone it at all, and neither do I. But Bud would discover that it was part of the culture of west Texas.

> **If you wanted to be cool in Bud's town, you had to go cruising.**

Every Friday and Saturday evening after dinner, the cars assembled in the center of town—marked by the only intersection with an honest-to-goodness traffic light. There were plenty of stop signs in town. Yield signs too. But a traffic light was a singular sight to behold.

In his early teens, Bud was a spectator, watching the cruisers cruise from his vantage point in front of the Boot Barn on Main Street, just a stone's throw away from the traffic light. He desperately wanted to become a cruiser, but cruising was by invitation only. And it was apparent that every car's dance card was full.

"It was like that for a full school year," Bud recalled with a sigh. Spots in cars usually opened up only when someone graduated.

After what felt like forever, "Pomp and Circumstance" caused opportunity to knock. There was more than one available vehicle open that year, but Bud cast his eyes on a 1963 Chevy Impala. "They invited me to take their open spot in the backseat," Bud said. "But whoever had been in the middle decided to slide over, so I was in the middle of the backseat surrounded by upperclassmen. Hey, it was jim-dandy with me 'cause I was just tickled to get any ol' seat!"

On his first Friday-night cruise, Bud quickly learned that cruising isn't real cruising unless you drink.

After the six guys got into the Impala, three in the front, three in the back, the first stop was the convenience store. A red-haired senior named Franky disappeared inside to buy beer. Franky had a fake ID and nerves of steel.

Bud had never had a drop of alcohol in his life. He had no idea what it tasted like, but just the thought of it gave him knots in the pit of his stomach.

"What's Franky getting?" Bud asked cautiously.

"Beer."

"How much beer?" Bud continued.

"A six-pack," they said in unison.

*Whew.* Bud exhaled. *I guess I can handle one can of beer.*

When Franky returned to the Impala, he wasn't carrying a six-pack of beer. He was carrying 6 six-packs—one for each cruiser. Bud had to suck in lots of air at that moment to keep from throwing up.

The rules were announced: Each guy drank his own six-pack while cruising. As each can was drained, the drinker would roll down the window and throw the can out onto the road, creating a distinct *clink, clink, clink* of aluminum hitting asphalt.

"Illegal drinking *and* flagrant littering," Bud would later emphasize. "It shoulda been more than a good boy could handle—but I still had a ways to go," he said, grimacing. If he closed his eyes, Bud could still taste that first gulp. "I took my first swig and almost choked to death," he remembered. "It was so bitter, so distasteful. I couldn't hardly stomach it."

But he wasn't going to admit it. He knew that if he didn't go along with the other five guys, they would call him all sorts of names, which was bad enough. But he would also most likely be kicked out of the car, the ultimate punishment.

Thinking fast, Bud devised a way to "drink" the beer without actually drinking the beer. "I like to call it backwash," Bud would say ever so smoothly and slowly.

Here's how it worked: Bud watched his cruising mates' intricate moves closely. Pop the tab on a beer can, swig until empty, throw the can out the window, and repeat. Bud would follow suit except each gulp he took was immediately spit back into his can. Bud timed his can toss simultaneously with his drinking buddies. There was one small problem, though. An empty beer can goes *clink, clink, clink*; a full beer can goes *clunk, clunk, clunk*. That made Bud nervous. He was certain the sound of his beer can would give him away. But whether it was the loud music and the whoopin' and hollerin' of all the other cruisers on the road or God Himself plugging up the other guys' ears, no one seemed to notice any difference.

Bud's ruse continued for a string of successive weekends. Meanwhile, his conscience was ready to erupt deep inside of him. He knew he was being hypocritical, participating in blatant lawbreaking. But the peer pressure was just too strong to resist.

> **Bud devised a way to "drink" a beer without actually drinking the beer.**

One Friday everything started out normally: rendezvous at the traffic light, stop and get beer, divvy up the six-packs, and then begin the slow cruise. But this night Bud felt courageous (or maybe it was insane) and decided to experiment. He would be the first one to throw his beer can out the car window. And so he did.

Bud's beer can went *clunk, clunk, clunk*, as his cans had each and every time before. Cringe, cringe, cringe went Bud's nerves. Without the cover of additional beer cans, the sound of his can seemed to be especially loud.

*Why don't these guys ever hear the difference?* Bud couldn't figure it out. *I can understand that later in the evening they are too drunk to realize what's going on. But this early in the parade, I would think they could figure it out!*

Now Bud zeroed in on the sounds of his friends' tossed cans. Wait! There were no *clink, clink, clinks*. They were going *clunk, clunk, clunk*.

No one was drinking the beer!

All six guys were part of an elaborate charade because none of them had the courage to stand up against the pressure.

Bud changed all that.

On Saturday night, Bud and his cruising buddies met at the center of town, jumped into the Impala, and drove to the convenience store. As Franky pulled out his fake ID and was just about to exit the car, Bud took a deep breath, swallowed hard, and then said, "Hey, Franky, tonight instead of beer, get me a six-pack of Dr. Pepper, okay?"

There was dead silence. Bud's five compadres froze. Did Bud just ask for a soft drink over beer? It was a three-second delay that seemed like an ice age. But then, one by one, every one of the cruisers chimed in. "Yeah, that sounds like a good idea. Make mine the same, Franky!"

It had taken courage, but Bud had successfully broken this chain of male bonding. By standing up for what he knew was right, he expressed exactly what all the other guys had been thinking all along but had been too afraid to voice.

In honor of Bud, a role model extraordinaire, I add courage to the Short List.

THE FOURTH IMPORTANT THING:

## Courage

I hope you enjoyed Bud's story of cruising in west Texas. But there's a better-known story of a teenager standing up against peer pressure and exhibiting incredible courage in the Old Testament:

David and Goliath. It's such a familiar story that most people think they know all the details backward and forward. Young teen armed with a slingshot and five stones kills heavily armored taunting giant. Said teen would later become the greatest king of Israel.

But in looking at the account more closely, I found a great deal of personal encouragement. It's a wonderful slice of historical courage in action.

I love the way the New Living Translation recounts the story in 1 Samuel 17:1-51.

> The Philistines now mustered their army for battle and camped between Socoh in Judah and Azekah at Ephes-dammim. Saul countered by gathering his Israelite troops near the valley of Elah. So the Philistines and Israelites faced each other on opposite hills, with the valley between them.
>
> Then Goliath, a Philistine champion from Gath, came out of the Philistine ranks to face the forces of Israel. He was over nine feet tall! He wore a bronze helmet, and his bronze coat of mail weighed 125 pounds. He also wore bronze leg armor, and he carried a bronze javelin on his shoulder. The shaft of his spear was as heavy and thick as a weaver's beam, tipped with an iron spearhead that weighed 15 pounds. His armor bearer walked ahead of him carrying a shield.
>
> Goliath stood and shouted a taunt across to the Israelites. "Why are you all coming out to fight?" he called. "I am the Philistine champion, but you are only the servants of Saul. Choose one man to come down here and fight me! If he kills me, then we will be your slaves. But if I kill him, you will be our slaves! I defy the armies of Israel today! Send me a man who will fight me!" When Saul and the Israelites heard this, they were terrified and deeply shaken.
>
> Now David was the son of a man named Jesse, an Ephrathite from Bethlehem in the land of Judah. Jesse was an old man at that time, and he had eight sons. Jesse's three oldest sons—Eliab, Abinadab, and Shimea—had already

joined Saul's army to fight the Philistines. David was the youngest son. David's three oldest brothers stayed with Saul's army, but David went back and forth so he could help his father with the sheep in Bethlehem.

For forty days, every morning and evening, the Philistine champion strutted in front of the Israelite army.

One day Jesse said to David, "Take this basket of roasted grain and these ten loaves of bread, and carry them quickly to your brothers. And give these ten cuts of cheese to their captain. See how your brothers are getting along, and bring back a report on how they are doing." David's brothers were with Saul and the Israelite army at the valley of Elah, fighting against the Philistines.

So David left the sheep with another shepherd and set out early the next morning with the gifts, as Jesse had directed him. He arrived at the camp just as the Israelite army was leaving for the battlefield with shouts and battle cries. Soon the Israelite and Philistine forces stood facing each other, army against army. David left his things with the keeper of supplies and hurried out to the ranks to greet his brothers. As he was talking with them, Goliath, the Philistine champion from Gath, came out from the Philistine ranks. Then David heard him shout his usual taunt to the army of Israel.

As soon as the Israelite army saw him, they began to run away in fright. "Have you seen the giant?" the men asked. "He comes out each day to defy Israel. The king has offered a huge reward to anyone who kills him. He will give that man one of his daughters for a wife, and the man's entire family will be exempted from paying taxes!"

David asked the soldiers standing nearby, "What will a man get for killing this Philistine and ending his defiance of Israel? Who is this pagan Philistine anyway, that he is allowed to defy the armies of the living God?"

And these men gave David the same reply. They said, "Yes, that is the reward for killing him."

But when David's oldest brother, Eliab, heard David talking to the men, he was angry. "What are you doing around here anyway?" he demanded. "What about those few sheep you're supposed to be taking care of? I know about your pride and deceit. You just want to see the battle!"

"What have I done now?" David replied. "I was only asking a question!" He walked over to some others and asked them the same thing and received the same answer. Then David's question was reported to King Saul, and the king sent for him.

"Don't worry about this Philistine," David told Saul. "I'll go fight him!"

"Don't be ridiculous!" Saul replied. "There's no way you can fight this Philistine and possibly win! You're only a boy, and he's been a man of war since his youth."

But David persisted. "I have been taking care of my father's sheep and goats," he said. "When a lion or a bear comes to steal a lamb from the flock, I go after it with a club and rescue the lamb from its mouth. If the animal turns on me, I catch it by the jaw and club it to death. I have done this to both lions and bears, and I'll do it to this pagan

Philistine, too, for he has defied the armies of the living God! The LORD who rescued me from the claws of the lion and the bear will rescue me from this Philistine!"

Saul finally consented. "All right, go ahead," he said. "And may the LORD be with you!"

Then Saul gave David his own armor—a bronze helmet and a coat of mail. David put it on, strapped the sword over it, and took a step or two to see what it was like, for he had never worn such things before.

"I can't go in these," he protested to Saul. "I'm not used to them." So David took them off again. He picked up five smooth stones from a stream and put them into his shepherd's bag. Then, armed only with his shepherd's staff and sling, he started across the valley to fight the Philistine.

Goliath walked out toward David with his shield bearer ahead of him, sneering in contempt at this ruddy-faced boy. "Am I a dog," he roared at David, "that you come at me with a stick?" And he cursed David by the names of his gods. "Come over here, and I'll give your flesh to the birds and wild animals!" Goliath yelled.

David replied to the Philistine, "You come to me with sword, spear, and javelin, but I come to you in the name of the LORD of Heaven's Armies—the God of the armies of Israel, whom you have defied. Today the LORD will conquer you, and I will kill you and cut off your head. And then I will give the dead bodies of your men to the birds and wild animals, and the whole world will know that there is a God in Israel! And everyone assembled here will know that the

LORD rescues his people, but not with sword and spear. This is the LORD's battle, and he will give you to us!"

As Goliath moved closer to attack, David quickly ran out to meet him. Reaching into his shepherd's bag and taking out a stone, he hurled it with his sling and hit the Philistine in the forehead. The stone sank in, and Goliath stumbled and fell face down on the ground.

So David triumphed over the Philistine with only a sling and a stone, for he had no sword. Then David ran over and pulled Goliath's sword from its sheath. David used it to kill him and cut off his head.   1 SAMUEL 17:1-51

Isn't this an incredible story of God's power and faithfulness, and the humble courage of a brave young man? Let's get a better handle on the two main characters in this historical account, beginning with Goliath.

### The Giant's Stats

We all know that Goliath was big and strong—a giant—but the text actually says how big and strong he really was!

He was over nine feet tall!   1 SAMUEL 17:4

In Hebrew writings, Goliath was said to be six cubits and one span tall; in the Dead Sea Scrolls and Greek versions, it is recorded that Goliath was four cubits and one span tall. Biblical scholars can't agree on exactly what the dimension of a cubit is. Based on my personal research, I have concluded that Goliath's height, based on a broad range of cubit size, would have been somewhere between nine feet six inches and nine feet nine inches tall! The footnote in the New Living Translation clarifies that the number is most likely around 9.75 feet, which is nine feet nine inches.

> **Goliath was tall. Tall, as in looking down on Shaquille O'Neal or Yao Ming.**

Let's face it. Goliath was tall.

Tall, as in looking down on Shaquille O'Neal or Yao Ming. That tall.

Courage is one of my favorite topics to present at men's retreats, and consequently I often tell the story of David and Goliath. When I mention Goliath's height, I feel compelled to bring in a visual aid.

I invite an average-sized guy up on stage with me. Typically, he is about six feet tall and weighs 185 pounds. The audience can see that we are almost the same height—give or take an inch—a pretty even match. (We won't talk about the weight.)

I pull up a wooden stool, and—rather than sitting down—I stand on it. Not only does standing on a stool make me tall, but I also love to see how people react when I am climbing up on top of it! Since most stools aren't all that sturdy, standing on one has incredible dramatic effect. (Of course, I always check it out in advance backstage before I actually do it onstage.) Voilá! I am a little over nine feet tall. It's very clear that for the guy standing next to me, this is not a fair fight. The odds are that I could cream this guy!

Okay, now that we know how big Goliath was, let's look at his armor, which attests to his strength.

> He wore a bronze helmet, and his bronze coat of mail weighed 125 pounds.   1 SAMUEL 17:5

Depending on your idea of what a shekel weighed in David's time, Goliath's armor weighed anywhere from 125 pounds on the light side to almost 200 pounds on the heavy side. Essentially, Goliath wore the weight of another human being on his back!

To illustrate the weighty point in my presentation, I ask my volunteer to jump on my back, piggyback style. I can hold him for a few minutes, as most men can. (For comic relief, I sometimes tell the man who is on my back that I am going to climb up on the wooden stool again and begin moving in its direction. I've heard from audience members many times that the look on my passenger's face was worth the price of admission to one of these weekend events.)

To further emphasize Goliath's strength, the text describes the giant warrior's spear:

> The shaft of his spear was as heavy and thick as a weaver's beam, tipped with an iron spearhead that weighed 15 pounds.   1 SAMUEL 17:7

Once again, based on how you convert the weight of a shekel to a pound, fifteen pounds is a conservative estimate of its weight. I believe Goliath's spearhead weighed between fifteen and twenty pounds. That doesn't seem incredibly heavy, but once again a visual aid helps bring home the point.

In my presentation, I find a freestanding microphone, take the microphone off the stand (carefully placing it somewhere safe), and then hoist the microphone stand like a spear. If it is an older microphone stand, it has a weighted round base that serves as my illustrative spearhead.

I continue talking with my spear poised, but it's not too long before my spearhead substitute begins drooping down toward the floor. Even a man with my great strength cannot hold that much weight aloft for an indefinite length of time. Goliath was stronger because *he* could.

We've touched on Goliath's physical prowess. Now let's become profilers and get inside Goliath's head.

### *A Giant Chunk on His Shoulder*

Goliath was anything but a shy, retiring, timid sort of fellow. No, Goliath definitely had an attitude.

In this story the first words out of his mouth are intimidating and full of mockery:

> Goliath stood and shouted a taunt across to the Israelites. "Why are you all coming out to fight?" he called. "I am the Philistine champion, but you are only the servants of Saul. Choose one man to come down here and fight me! . . . I defy the armies of Israel today! Send me a man who will fight me!" 1 SAMUEL 17:8, 10

I don't know what the Hebrew word is for "trash-talking," but that is exactly what was going on here. "Na, na, na, na, na, na—who is gonna fight me?" For some of us, those words bring a flashback to a playground with our childhood friends, hearing the constant taunting of the school-yard bully. Of course, Goliath's bravado was heightened by the fact that no one from Israel's army was courageous enough to go out there and stand up against him.

Next, we see that Goliath was relentless. Did you pick that characteristic up when you read the text?

> For forty days, every morning and evening, the Philistine champion strutted in front of the Israelite army.
> 1 SAMUEL 17:16

So this guy was a taunter. He mocked. He intimidated. What could be worse? How about that he did it every day and every night for almost a month and a half? Imagine your next-door neighbor standing across the fence and cursing you loudly nonstop, morning and night. Okay, maybe you could tolerate it for one day, but what if he did it again the next day? And on and on for six weeks! Talk about being beaten down verbally.

Goliath was more than just a physical giant. He was a giant pain in the neck! But there is one other characteristic of Goliath that you may have overlooked. For a lot of us, it is the most crucial point in dealing with our own personal giants.

Goliath was outside of a relationship with God. David hit a bull's-eye when he posed the question:

> "Who is this *pagan* Philistine anyway, that he is allowed to defy the armies of the living God?"
> 1 SAMUEL 17:26, EMPHASIS ADDED

Many of us see the word *pagan* and think of an unbeliever, someone outside the family of God. The literal translation of the Hebrew word used here means "uncircumcised."

"Uncircumcised" had less to do with the physical surgery on a baby boy and more to do with the fact that circumcision was an outward symbol that these boys would be true to the one true God, Jehovah.

Goliath was an unbeliever. As I write these words, I think of many of my friends who are enduring difficult times right now, suffering some sort of abuse at the hands of people outside the family of God. One friend is specifically targeted because he is a Christian. The unbeliever in his life has something against believers; something ugly happened to this man years before he met my friend, but he is fully set in his quest to make my friend's life miserable. It isn't fair, but it is the way life can go.

> **Goliath was a physical giant and a giant pain in the neck! But lest we forget, Goliath was also an unbeliever.**

What does my friend need in order to withstand this abuse? Courage.

And it is courage that is personified in the life of our story's hero, David. Let's take a closer look.

### David

The first thing we notice about David is that he was a shepherd:

> But David went back and forth so he could help his father with the sheep in Bethlehem. 1 SAMUEL 17:15

> **David's advantage against Goliath wasn't in his natural abilities but in his power from the Lord and David's courage to use it.**

I am no expert on the world of shepherding. Growing up in Philadelphia, I was not really surrounded by men and women who pursued shepherding as their careers. Consequently, I take a lot of heat from the shepherds of the world for my rather dull view of their profession.

Even though shepherds must have many important skills, the bottom-line description of a shepherd in my little brain is basically people who babysit sheep.

Okay, okay, maybe that's a little flippant, but reading between the lines brings me to this conclusion: David wasn't even the shepherd in charge; Jesse, his father, was the main man. To me, the lower you go on the organizational chart, the more you look like a babysitter.

Okay, okay, I know David killed wild animals with his bare hands in order to protect the sheep, but mind you, that didn't happen every day. My point is this: David was not "preparing" for his battle with Goliath by being a shepherd, any more than you and I are "preparing" to fight our giants by spending a little more time each day on our laptop. David's advantage was not in his natural abilities but in his power from the Lord and his courage to use it.

Second, David was a musician. We learn that bit of information from the previous chapter in 1 Samuel:

> One of the servants said to Saul, "One of Jesse's sons from Bethlehem is a talented harp player." 1 SAMUEL 16:18

Now that I have all the shepherds angry at me, I might as well go for the gold and get all the musicians mad at me as well. This is especially tough since I have quite a few musicians in my own immediate family—but here goes.

David knew how to tickle the strings on a harp. There's no doubt that he had talent. But what picture does that conjure up in your mind? Is this the guy you want representing your country in the fight against a giant?

Let's put it in today's world. The president of the United States announces from the Oval Office that the government has discovered the secret location of one of the highest-ranking terrorist leaders in the world. He must be taken out, destroyed, done away with. "Therefore," the president continues, "I am asking for all of my fellow Americans who play the flute to assemble immediately at Camp Pendleton in California so we can create a crack task force of the best soldiers to take out this enemy."

Are you going to sleep more soundly tonight, knowing that the president has a bunch of flute players protecting us from harm?

You get my point.

So David is a shepherd and a musician. And where does he fall in his family birth order? He's the baby.

David was the youngest son.    1 SAMUEL 17:14

I'm not a huge believer in the birth order concepts that many psychologists tout in their books—probably because I've seen as many exceptions to the rules as perfect matches. But nonetheless, it is a fascinating study in human behavior.

Those who are oldest are naturally called firstborns. They are characterized as having self-confidence, natural leadership characteristics, and competitive spirits. They also are high achievers. The seven astronauts chosen for NASA's original Mercury space program were all firstborns. Many Fortune 500 CEOs are firstborns, attesting to their natural leadership abilities.

If you are neither the oldest nor the youngest, you are

the middle child. You are known to be a great negotiator and possess good social skills—in other words, you are a mediator who is very understanding. But one middle-child characteristic that really stands out for me is fierce competitiveness. Why would a middle child compete so fiercely? Ask one. "I hate being in my older sister's shadow, so I'm gonna make a name for myself!" Or "I don't care that my older brother was the star of the football team. I'm gonna break every one of his records plus play baseball—which he was lousy at!"

And then we have the youngest—the babies. Since their parents have already had other children, Mom and Dad are getting more relaxed in their parenting style, and the lastborn is more laid-back and relaxed too. Babies in the birth order can suffer from low self-esteem because they feel they can never measure up to all their older siblings. But my favorite attribute of lastborns is summed up in their oft-used expression: "Take care of me!"

They've got it made! Older brothers and sisters were put on earth to meet their every need. "Change my diaper, make me breakfast, do my homework, fight my battles!"

Are you paying attention? David was the baby. It sure seems to me that he would be the last one anyone would consider as the giant killer.

That's my point. I apologize profusely for angering all you shepherds, musicians, and youngest children, but added together, these attributes made David a very unlikely candidate for hero. Some of us can fantasize this story into a blockbuster movie with the role of David being played by Daniel Day-Lewis or Brad Pitt. I don't think it was that way. In fact, I believe David was pretty much like me. Not a superstar, but an average Joe. And an average Joe who knows his or her power source and has the courage to use it can win every time.

Do you want to be more courageous? What does a courageous person look like today, based on David's profile? I see four timeless principles in this account.

### A Courageous Person Takes the Initiative

As you were reading the story, did you notice how David was the one guy who eventually stood up to take on the frightening task?

> David asked the soldiers standing nearby, "What will a man get for killing this Philistine and ending his defiance of Israel? Who is this pagan Philistine anyway, that he is allowed to defy the armies of the living God?"
> 1 SAMUEL 17:26

Essentially, David was saying, "Well, it doesn't look like anyone else is going to stand up to this guy, but somebody's got to take the initiative. By the way, what's the reward for giant killing this year?"

For twenty-five preceding verses in this story, no one took the lead! Since Goliath was challenging the Israelites for at least forty days, that's a lot of sitting around and passing the buck.

But David demonstrated incredible courage by doing something different from all his fellow Israelites—including his brothers. It's kind of like my west Texas friend, Bud, showing courage by ordering Dr. Pepper instead of beer. Instead of doing the same ole same ole, a courageous person is willing to push the envelope, think outside the box, and take a stand for what is right and what really should be done.

> **A courageous person is willing to push the envelope and take a stand for what is right and what really should be done.**

Take heart if you need this specific encouragement right now. Maybe you have been trapped in a bad situation for a long time, but because everyone else around you is in the same trap, you have lacked the positive peer pressure to break free from its chains. God says you can be victorious over your adversity, over your addiction, over your sin if you just show the courage to stand up against it. You may be alone, but remember, you're never really completely alone, for our Lord walks with each of us every moment of every day.

There's a second characteristic of a courageous person.

### A Courageous Person Learns How to Handle Criticism

The irony of this point amazes me. King Saul finally had a volunteer who was willing to stand up to Goliath. Granted,

David was not the physical specimen the king had in mind, and rather than being grateful and encouraging, Saul gave David a pretty stinging critique:

> "Don't worry about this Philistine," David told Saul. "I'll go fight him!"
> "Don't be ridiculous!" Saul replied. "There's no way you can fight this Philistine and possibly win! You're only a boy, and he's been a man of war since his youth."
> 1 SAMUEL 17:32-33

What's going on here? The first point about a courageous person taking the initiative sounds so cool, so inviting, so brave, yet once David does it, the first thing he runs into is a barrage of criticism.

In my simplistic little mind, there are basically two kinds of people in this world: people who like criticism and people who don't. Those who like criticism offer it freely to each and every person they come in contact with. They don't see themselves as doing anything wrong; their critiques are given to strengthen the person whom they are critiquing. Naturally, often these people can handle the criticism of others much more easily than their polar opposites—people who are crushed by criticism.

For them, every critique is a balloon buster. They avoid criticism like the plague, and of course, they never dole out critiques to others in any circumstance.

If critics only critiqued each other and left the rest of

us alone, there would be less tension in our world. But like a tracking device, critics zero in on people who abhor criticism and dump their "wisdom" on them anyway. For the people in the former group, I would refer you back to page 52 for a refresher on how to speak the truth in love with tact.) If you have difficulty dealing with criticism, perhaps David can be a role model for you. He developed thick skin and was able to handle the criticism with courage. He then passed this quality on to his children, as echoed in his son King Solomon's words:

> Whoever stubbornly refuses to accept criticism
> will suddenly be destroyed beyond recovery.
> PROVERBS 29:1

As we get to the heart of David and Goliath's story, we see another key attribute of a courageous person.

## A Courageous Person Is Victorious in His or Her Own Way

Pay careful attention to the next scene:

> Then Saul gave David his own armor—a bronze helmet and a coat of mail. David put it on, strapped the sword over it, and took a step or two to see what it was like, for he had never worn such things before.
> "I can't go in these," he protested to Saul. "I'm not used to them." So David took them off again. He picked up five smooth stones from a stream and put them into

his shepherd's bag. Then, armed only with his shepherd's staff and sling, he started across the valley to fight the Philistine.    1 SAMUEL 17:38-40

Because we are all so familiar with this account, we may miss the absolute incredulity of David's action. David refused to fight with a sword or armor; instead, he decided to dump the king's armor and just pack a slingshot!

Again, maybe a modernized illustration would help.

> **If God has called you to do something in a way that has never been done before, He will give you the victory.**

If you were in charge of the U.S. military sending our men and women off to war today, what weapons would you make available to them? "We're gonna beat this enemy," you announce to your troops. "So everyone pick up your own top-of-the-line personal peashooter and let's go win a war!"

Ludicrous. That's exactly how the Israelite army must have felt when David faced off with Goliath carrying his slingshot.

The beautiful principle illustrated here is that if God has called you to do something in a way that has never been done before, He will give you the victory no matter how it may look to others.

Think how things in our world would not have advanced if there had been no change from how it had been done before. We would still be reading by candlelight, communicating by smoke signals, and living in caves.

Or think about it in ministry terms. Someone had to step forward and try doing church with a contemporary band instead of a choir and an organ so that folks would have more than one option for worship. Someone had to say, "Let's create an organization specifically designed to reach teenagers with the gospel" before any parachurch youth agency was ever conceived. Someone had to create missionary organizations, small-group discipleship curriculum, retreat and conference centers for people to reflect on their spiritual life.

Get my point? All of these things were started somewhere in time by a person or persons who had a calling from God different from any other person before them. Their styles were different yet appropriate, so God chose to bless them.

What is God calling you to do that has never been done before? Are you courageous enough to move on it? Take your cue from David and act on your leading, moving in the power of God.

That's underscored in the last principle of courage.

### *A Courageous Person Knows the Power Is from the Lord*

This is the crux of the story. Why was David able to defeat the giant in his life? Because he understood his power source. It was not by his strength that the battle was won but by the power of God.

> David replied to the Philistine, "You come to me with sword, spear, and javelin, but I come to you in the name of the LORD

of Heaven's Armies—the God of the armies of Israel, whom you have defied. Today the LORD will conquer you, and I will kill you and cut off your head. . . . This is the LORD's battle, and he will give you to us!"   1 SAMUEL 17:45-47

When I learn to trust God for my power, I display true courage. All the other principles fall short if I don't put this one in play. I can be an initiator. I can handle criticism. I can even approach my giant in a different way than ever before. But if God's not in it, the victory is not for certain.

You will always confront foes who appear stronger. You will always see people who appear more courageous. But take hold of this promise: if you trust God, turn the battle over to Him, and surrender yourself to Him, He will give you the victory.

I can really relate to David. Physically, he wasn't the poster child of courage. Neither am I. Maybe you feel the same way. But I've got good news.

God sees it differently.

# The Lesson from My Father

The phone call came early one Saturday evening in August 1996. It was my younger sister, Dale, and she was almost hysterical. "Dad had a severe heart attack while he was out playing miniature golf. He was given CPR and taken to the hospital by the paramedics. That's all I know."

After calming her down, I was able to retrieve a little more information, like what hospital Dad was in. "Let me see if I can get someone on the phone who can tell me a little more about what's going on," I said to Dale.

If you drew a line on a map connecting my sister's, my dad's, and my homes, you would end up with a big triangle: there was a lot of geography between us. Dad lived in Pennsylvania, my sister lived in Florida, and I lived in California.

I called the hospital. First, I was transferred to the emergency room. Then I was put on hold because "We want you to speak to a doctor." Thankfully the hold time was kept to a minimum. "Hello, Mr. Butterworth, this is Dr. Jones." Jones wasn't actually the doctor's last name, but with all the crazy thoughts swimming around in my brain, I didn't catch the real one. I did catch two things immediately: she was a woman and didn't sound like she grew up in Philly or Pennsylvania or any of the fifty states for that matter.

"I examined your father in the emergency room when the paramedics brought him in a little over an hour ago."

"Yes?" I replied, not really knowing what to say.

"Mr. Butterworth, I am sorry to have to tell you that your father has passed away."

I'm sure I responded right away, but my mind suddenly felt like someone hit the "Hold" button on my life's DVR. "What happened?"

"It appears to have been a massive heart attack. According to his friend, Bob Lawhead, who accompanied the paramedics, your father was out with some friends playing miniature golf. Midway through the game, he bent over to putt, looked back up at his friend, said, 'Oh my!' and collapsed. He dropped like a rock, hitting his head on the ground with such force that his forehead began bleeding." She paused, then added kindly, "But I am fairly certain,

Mr. Butterworth, your father died before he ever hit the ground."

I was unable to speak. In her defense, the doctor was neither cold nor insensitive, yet the matter-of-fact tone in her voice convinced me she had no idea who she was talking about. This was my dad.

"The paramedics were summoned as soon as he collapsed," she continued. "They were unable to resuscitate him. They found no pulse. He was admitted into the hospital at 10:28 p.m., having already been given CPR for thirty minutes. He had no heartbeat for thirty-five to forty minutes. He was pronounced dead at 10:31 p.m. By law we are required to call a medical examiner to look into this case. But it is very straightforward. There will be no autopsy required."

We shared more information, mostly regarding the transportation of my dad's body from the hospital to a funeral home. I explained to her that I lived on the West Coast and would do my best to keep things moving as quickly as possible. "Whatever you can do we would appreciate," she replied. Then she added, "But we understand you need some time. Do what you need to do. We'll wait to hear from you. I am so sorry for your loss."

I hung up the phone. By now the sun had set and I was sitting in darkness, but I didn't notice. In the shadows, I redialed my sister's number. "Dale, Dad is gone," I said, trying not to break down, knowing full well she would.

Our plan was to get to Philadelphia as soon as we

could. I told Dale I would handle all the funeral home arrangements and asked if she would contact Dad's church.

I knew there was nothing either of us could do until Monday morning.

I was a divorced, single dad at the time, so I let my five children know, two of whom were away at college. They all handled it just like their dad initially . . . stunned disbelief and silence.

> **My mom was a good woman, but my dad was my hero.**

We had gone through this before when my mother had died several years earlier.

But that experience was different for me altogether. My mom was a good woman, but I was never close to her. On the other hand, my dad was my hero.

◆◆◆◆

Born April 18, 1921, in northeast Philadelphia, my dad, William Jesse Butterworth, grew up in a solid blue-collar family of railroad workers. The railroad defined my family. My grandfather was an electrician for the Reading Railroad, carrying a company loyalty that he would pass on to my father. Dad worked forty-one years for the Reading Railroad, starting as a freight car cleaner, moving up the ladder to freight car mechanic, then on to assistant foreman of the car shop, and ultimately to the top position of general foreman.

His younger brother, my uncle Joe, worked in the ticket office of the historic Reading Terminal on Twelfth and Market Streets in downtown Philadelphia. My mom worked at the Reading Terminal too—that's where she and my dad met. Her dad, my maternal grandfather, held the ultimate railroad job—he was an engineer whose experience went back to the steam-locomotive days, the Iron Horse era. (In order to keep the family tradition alive, I worked on the railroad too—for one summer during my high school years. Those few weeks of entry-level service were enough to convince me something had not been passed along in the family gene pool.)

In many ways, I was a typical child growing up in the United States in the fifties and sixties. Dad worked long hours, and Mom stayed home to cook and clean and raise my sister and me. I spent more time with my mom, but I treasured the time I had with my dad. I remember our evening meals together. The menu was nothing fancy. We ate a lot of hot dogs, ground beef, and spaghetti. We didn't talk much; our top priority was food intake. (Did I mention we all tended toward being overweight?)

After dinner on Saturdays, we'd all take our showers or baths for church the next morning; put on pajamas, robes, and slippers; then hustle back downstairs to gather around the television. Nothing could disrupt my dad and mom from watching their favorite program—*The Lawrence Welk Show*. Mom would dish up a treat for us—a bowl of vanilla ice cream dripping with chocolate syrup and topped off by two small pretzels. It was heaven.

Dad and Mom grew up listening to the big bands on

the radio. Lawrence Welk held the final baton of a dying phenomenon. My parents fell in love dancing and singing to Tommy Dorsey, Jimmy Dorsey, Benny Goodman, Kay Kyser, Artie Shaw, and their personal favorite, Glenn Miller. As a young boy I remember going with my family to Atlantic City in the summertime, not to hang out at the beach, but to go to Steel Pier, where aging big bands played nightly at ten in the ballroom. My sister and I would sit unattended by the bandstand while Dad and Mom danced away their worries, trying to recapture the romance of their youth.

> **Dad and Mom grew up listening to the big bands on the radio—especially their personal favorite, Glenn Miller.**

When they couldn't be at Steel Pier during the rest of the year, Saturday night at nine transported my parents back in time without ever leaving their living room. Dad had played the saxophone in high school, so he was particularly fond of that section in the band. Every Saturday evening he drilled me on the elements of every big band sax section. Two alto saxophones, two tenor saxophones, and one big baritone saxophone. That was perfection. Occasionally one of the five guys would place his primary sax in its stand and pick up the soprano sax, which looked like a golden clarinet. And of course, each of the sax players could play the clarinet as well. But two altos, two tenors, and a bari—that was the traditional way and Dad's favorite.

I was too young at the time to realize how odd it was for a young person to enjoy Lawrence Welk. All I knew was my dad enjoyed him, and Dad's endorsement was all I ever needed.

On Sunday morning we would wake up and prepare for Sunday school and the morning church service. I was always ready before my parents, so I would scurry outside to get the Sunday edition of the *Philadelphia Inquirer* waiting on the front step. It was the only day of the week we had the paper delivered, and I thought walking a few steps out the door to get the paper was pretty amazing. Removing the thick, white string that held all the sections of the thick paper together, I would find and read the funnies, then scan the sports page if the Phillies were playing.

Eventually Dad and Mom would come down the stairs, the strong smell of perfume and aftershave blending together into one pungent aromatic cloud that preceded them. Mom would be in a pretty church dress, and Dad would be decked out in a sport coat and tie. I loved to see Dad dressed up. For many years, his signature fashion statement was a matching tie and pocket square. Occasionally he would wear a set of cuff links with a matching tie clasp. He had several options tucked away in his tiny jewelry box—all trains. Gold trains, silver trains, steam engines, diesel locomotives, all trains. I thought Dad always looked sharp for church. He explained that, after all, he was an usher, so he wanted to look his best when he guided people to their favorite pews.

When church was over, we would drive home, change clothes, and Mom would finish making Sunday dinner. On Monday through Saturday, we ate our big meal around 5:30 p.m. and called it supper; on Sunday, we ate at 2 p.m. and called it dinner.

Honoring the commandment of resting on the Sabbath, we would nap, read the paper, and just sneak a peek at the TV to see how badly the Eagles were losing. We didn't watch the whole game because there was "no TV watching on the Lord's Day." It was back to church on Sunday night. Apparently the Lord's Day officially ended at 8 p.m. because when we returned home we were allowed to watch *The Ed Sullivan Show*, ending the weekend all too soon.

I didn't see a lot of Dad Monday through Friday. And Saturday he tackled a long list of "honey do's" from Mom before being swept onto the dance floor with Lawrence Welk's music.

Even more than watching *The Lawrence Welk Show* together, I looked forward to my favorite day of the year with my dad: Thanksgiving. Turkey Day was the one day of the year when I could go to work with my dad. Dad hated that he had to work on holidays, so he would usually do his best to swing some deals with his coworkers so he could be home on Christmas. As part of the trade-off, he worked Thanksgiving.

It was a light day on the railroad, especially for moving freight, so Dad could always make it home for a

Thanksgiving feast around 3 p.m. He would begin work at 7 a.m., meaning we were up even earlier than usual. I watched my dad eat his bowl of cornflakes and drink his cup of black coffee while I ate toast with lots of jelly. I don't know what inspired him to take me on that first crisp autumn morning. (The "take your kids to work" idea hadn't been introduced yet.)

I know I was young—maybe six or seven—and this continued for another five or six years. Dad may have done it just to spend some time with me. Or he may have done it to cut my mom some slack since she was busy getting the feast ready and wouldn't have to keep an eye on me. I don't know why he started doing this, but I'm certainly glad he did.

> **My favorite day of the year with my dad was Thanksgiving, when I could go to work with him at the freight yard.**

We would drive together in the family car—a black 1957 Ford Fairlane. We'd arrive at the Port Richmond freight yard, and Dad would begin his daily ritual of "walking the yard," as he called it. After the walk, we'd head into his office—an old redbrick building flanked by freight cars on tracks on the one side and the cold, dirty Delaware River on the other side. Dad's office was a small room on the second floor of the building. It was far from immaculate, imposing, or impressive. But it was where my dad worked, so I considered it hallowed ground. It smelled musty and looked like a warehouse for stacks of official railroad paperwork. You could definitely see the evidence of "working on freight cars and getting your hands greasy before coming back to the office to fill in a bunch of paperwork" on everything there.

Usually it was a light crew on that fourth Thursday in November. Sometimes a couple of other guys were in the office, too, but I always treasured the few occasions when it was just me and my dad. He would sit in a squeaky chair at an ancient wooden desk, filling out reports on clipboards, reading other coworkers' reports, and scanning official railroad memoranda. I was given the copilot's seat—the small desk over in the corner where the highest-tech gadget I had ever seen in my short life took up most of the space. It may have been the first love of my life.

I think I had a crush on an Underwood manual typewriter.

The Reading Railroad didn't deal in state-of-the-art equipment, so I am guessing this typewriter was made in the late 1930s or early '40s. Like all manual typewriters, it had a personality all its own, making it unique from all others. This particular machine had a cantankerous *S* key—it always struck the paper higher on the line than any of the other letters, adding its distinctive signature.

As Dad worked, I sat at a desk eight feet away from him. No words were uttered, and there were no sounds other than the random shuffle of papers, the *peck peck* of a little boy trying to type, the *hiss* of the old steam pipes heating the room, and the *tick, tick* of the wall clock's pendulum. It was the best of all worlds in my book. I loved it, because I loved being with my dad.

Before I knew it, the day had ended all too quickly and we were back in the Ford, driving home, making a quick stop at the local Horn & Hardart Automat to see if they had any pumpkin pies left to take home since Uncle Joe was usually a last-minute guest. On the way out of the restaurant, Dad would buy me a big, warm soft pretzel from the vendor on the street corner. I savored every bite on the drive home.

> **As Dad worked, I sat at a desk eight feet away from him. I loved it, because I loved being with my dad.**

I loved that day even though my dad and I barely spoke. I don't know why. As time passed, I realized I had mountains of questions I wished I could have asked him. But Dad and I didn't do that sort of thing. I accepted that fact and simply relished the opportunity to be near my father, in his presence.

The phone call from the hospital had brought all of that to a close.

♦♦♦♦

On Monday morning I finalized the arrangements with the funeral home for the memorial service and burial. Dale and Uncle Joe would fly up together from Florida, and my two oldest children would accompany me from California. We agreed to meet up at Dad's house in a couple of days. We planned to finish the funeral arrangements when we got there—choosing the coffin and taking care of any last-minute details.

While I was making all these arrangements back in California, I called Dale in Miami to check on her. She sounded better than I expected, but she uncovered a new dilemma when she was making arrangements with Dad's church. "We can have a small meal in the church basement after the graveside service," she reported. "Actually the church is taking care of everything with no charge."

"Wow, that's nice," I replied.

"They loved Dad at that church," Dale said slowly. I could hear the tears beginning to kick in.

"Everybody loved Dad" was all I could think of to say.

Dale cleared her throat. "But we have a little problem."

"What is it?"

"Well, with it being August, the pastor is on vacation and unavailable to conduct the services."

"That's a shame," I said to her. "What are our other options?"

"Well, they have other guys on the church staff—you know—young associate pastors who can do it. But none of them really knew Dad all that well."

"Is that what they suggested?"

"No. Actually they had another option they said we ought to consider."

"What is it?"

"They think you should do it."

"Me? Conduct my own father's funeral?"

"Yes." She paused, allowing the full force of that statement to settle in. I could hear Dale take a deep breath. "Bill, if you think you're up to it, I think you should do it too."

"Conduct my own father's funeral service," I repeated over and over. "I've never done a funeral before. I've done weddings, but I've never done a funeral before. This would be a rough one to start with."

"It would mean a lot to Dad." My sister had to up the ante.

My stomach was tensing up into a giant knot. *This is a bad idea. Too much pressure. Too much stress. I don't think I can do it without breaking down. I'll embarrass myself in front of friends and family. It's just not necessary.*

But a small voice whispered to me, "You should do it."

"I'll do it," I blurted out.

"You will?" My sister sounded startled.

"Yes. I don't want some young associate who didn't really know Dad do something this important. Call back the church and offer them this deal. I will do the memorial service if they can get one of their pastors who knew Dad to do the graveside service."

So that's how I ended up conducting my own father's funeral service.

I knew from the start that what I wanted more than anything was to pay tribute to my dad. What did my father model for me? What was it that he passed along to me? What was his legacy to me? These questions flooded my mind; suddenly I experienced a gut-wrenching twist in my abdomen. These were the very same questions I had worked through in a totally different context just a few years earlier.

Remember how this book began? I had to take a hard look at how my kids would remember me when my life on earth was complete. Now I was being asked to do the same thing in my relationship with my father.

It didn't fully hit me at the time, but I was connecting three generations of life. How I remembered my dad would greatly influence the way I would want to be remembered by my children and those around me. It was my youngest son's first words and my father's death that gave birth to the Short List—how a person should want to be remembered.

When I agreed to conduct my father's memorial service, I had no idea how emotional I would feel doing it—telling a roomful of people why my dad was my hero. The eulogy for my father was essentially a reading of his Short List. Granted, he didn't call it his Short List, but it perfectly described the man I looked up to. Yes, the emotion of the moment was palpable as I began my remarks.

I proudly recalled how *honest* my dad had always been. "An honest day's work for an honest day's pay" was a maxim by which my father lived. He wouldn't tolerate dishonesty, and early in my life he taught me to value the truth in its purest form. He wasn't a man who would have had a lot of room for "spin." His integrity was obvious, and he let me observe what he thought, what he saw, where he went, and what he did.

I learned a lot about *courage* from watching my dad too. A popular word in the vernacular of my father's generation, which had grown up during the Depression, was gumption. Get out there and make something of yourself; go out there and do something! For many men and women of that time, it required risk, taking the initiative, thinking outside the box. It also required courage. Of course, as part of the "Greatest Generation," he proudly displayed his courage by fighting for his country in World War II. I like to think of him as a modern-day David fighting his own Goliaths with strength, wisdom, and courage.

> **"**
>
> **Dad's integrity was obvious. He let me observe what he thought, what he saw, where he went, and what he did.**
>
> **"**

My dad was a real man of *faith*—a quiet, personal faith. He wasn't a charismatic personal evangelist who wore his love for Christ on his sleeve with fiery passion, but his faith was apparent and strong nonetheless. I know that we never missed a Sunday church service. Never. Dad's gift to the church wasn't to teach or preach; he was an usher and a trustee. In both positions, he really shined. Faith was not a fad to my dad. It was a lifelong commitment to the Lord he truly enjoyed serving.

But most of all, I got to tell everyone about my dad's *love*. He loved his life. He loved his job. He loved his wife.

He loved his Lord. He loved his kids. He loved me. He wasn't one to verbalize it all that much, but I never questioned it. I loved him and he loved me and that was that. He left me an unmistakable legacy.

I know there are many ways my dad could have improved. (Isn't that true for all of us?) But I truly believe he did the best he could with the gifts he had been given. His Short List was easy to see, and its effect will remain with me for the rest of my life.

None of us are perfect. But it's important not to allow the shortcomings of life to detour us from living out our Short List. When we haven't met our goals because of our sins, we confess our faults to God who offers us undeserved mercy and forgiveness. As we lean into His Spirit, His power and blessing will fill us.

I summed up my father's life by quoting a wonderful passage from the Gospel of Matthew. In it, the Lord Jesus described the Short List in one word: *serving*.

> But Jesus called them to Himself and said, "You know that the rulers of the Gentiles lord it over them, and their great men exercise authority over them. It is not this way among you, but whoever wishes to become great among you shall be your servant, and whoever wishes to be first among you shall be your slave; just as the Son of Man did not come to be served, but to serve, and to give His life a ransom for many." MATTHEW 20:25-28, NASB

My dad was not a headline maker like a president or a sports hero or a celebrity. His greatness wasn't defined by fame, but it was defined by service. He lived out his Short List without fanfare, deliberately and effectively. As his son, I couldn't have been prouder.

Yes, there was a powerful emotion inside of me that day. It didn't emanate from the crowd or the room or the occasion. The rush of emotion came as I realized I was standing eight feet away from my dad in his coffin. Once again, Dad and I were eight feet apart, but this time it wasn't at separate desks in a railroad office. And I had never felt closer.

> **None of us are too insignificant or too important for God's service.**

My dad's servant attitude carries a message for all of us. It doesn't matter what our position in life may be. God loves each one of us and wants you and me to live out our Short List wherever we are. So I encourage you to start thinking about your Short List—whatever your age. What would you include on it? You may choose different character traits than the ones I included on mine, but I'm sure we can agree upon one thing: None of us are too insignificant or too important for God's service.

The power of the Short List is that whatever we do, when it is accomplished with the servant attitude that Jesus exemplified, people around us see Him more clearly. That's a legacy we can all be proud to leave behind.

**Introduction: The Lesson from My Son's First Words**
1. Do you know the first words you said as a child? Do you have a fun story about one of your relatives or friends that revolves around a baby's first words?

2. Have you ever been impacted by the words of a child? Has a child ever said something to you in complete innocence that made a big difference in your life?

3. How do you want to be remembered by those closest to you? What do you consider to be the most important things in life? Could you put them in four words?

4. What was the most significant truth you learned from this chapter? What difference will it make in your life?

✦✦✦✦

## Chapter One: The Lesson from Little League

1. Do you have a humorous story from your childhood or youth that is built around "love"?

2. How would you have defined love when you were younger? How would you define it now? If your definition has changed significantly, what has been the catalyst for that change?

3. How does this story help us understand the concept that God loves us, even when we are unlovable?

4. What was the most significant truth you learned from this chapter? What difference will it make in your life?

✦✦✦✦

## The First Important Thing: Love

1. Faith, hope, and love—the greatest of these is love. Would you agree with that assessment, or do you see one of the other two qualities as more important?

2. Have you personally experienced a relationship in which love continued to grow? What were some of the signs that love was maturing?

3. Do you have someone "unlovable" in your life? How can God's love working through you make a difference in this situation?

4. What was the most significant truth you learned in this chapter? What difference will it make in your life?

♦ ♦ ♦ ♦

**Chapter Two: The Lesson from Fourth Period Chemistry**

1. Do you have a story (funny or otherwise) of getting caught doing something dishonest when you were younger? Like stealing a cookie from the cookie jar? cheating on a test? playing hooky from school?

2. For many people, it's easy to be honest in the big things yet dishonest in the little things. Why do you think that's often the case?

3. What is the most important lesson you would pass on to someone else about the necessity of being honest?

4. What was the most significant truth you learned from this chapter? What difference will it make in your life?

✦✦✦✦

**The Second Important Thing: Honesty**

1. What you think, what you say, what you see, where you walk, what you do—in which area are you the strongest? Which area presents the greatest struggle for you? How are you personally working to strengthen that area? How do you think you can improve?

2. If you had to choose one or the other, would you say you are more truthful or more loving by nature? What do you think you need to do to incorporate the other characteristic into your life?

3. Write down how you first became honest with God. Did trusting His truth set you free? How did that feel?

4. What was the most significant truth you learned from this chapter? What difference will it make in your life?

✦✦✦✦

**Chapter Three: The Lesson from Big Buttermobile**

1. Have you ever had a "roof of the car" incident occur in your own life? Has a family member or friend ever told you a "roof of the car" story?

2. This chapter illustrates how easy it is to be so focused on your own world that you neglect the feelings of others in your life. Have you had a similar issue in your life? How has this issue played itself out?

3. The character quality we're setting up with this chapter is faith. In your life, what's the most important thing you have learned about faith so far?

4. What was the most significant truth you learned in this chapter? What difference will it make?

♦♦♦♦

**The Third Important Thing: Faith**
1. It's not enough just to have faith in faith. You need to believe "the right stuff." Based on what you read in this chapter, what is the right stuff?

2. Your faith will require you to make changes in your life. Why is that so difficult for most people? Why are we resistant to change? How can we become more comfortable with it?

3. Are you facing a challenging season in your life right now? How has your faith helped you withstand crisis? What advice would you share with others about the value of faith in your life, specifically as it relates to dealing with pain?

4. What was the most significant truth you learned in this chapter? What difference will it make in your life?

♦ ♦ ♦ ♦

**Chapter Four: The Lesson from Cruising with the Doctor**
1. Have you ever been in a situation reminiscent of the cruising story recounted in this chapter? If you're comfortable doing so, share it with another person.

2. Do you have another story from your past that addresses the power of peer pressure? Have you ever done something just because everyone else was doing it?

3. Why is it so difficult to stand on one's own?

4. What was the most significant truth you learned in this chapter? What difference will it make in your life?

♦ ♦ ♦ ♦

**The Fourth Important Thing: Courage**
1. Which of the principles of courage spoke loudest to you in this chapter? How will you apply it to your life?

2. How do you tap into the power of the Lord? Explain in practical terms what that looks like in your life.

3. Is there a situation in your life right now that is requiring courage? Are you being asked to take the initiative in a circumstance that really seems to be God's leading? Are you being criticized? Find someone to share your thoughts with.

4. What was the most significant truth you learned in this chapter? What difference will it make in your life?

◆◆◆◆

## Afterword: The Lesson from My Father

1. If someone had to deliver the eulogy at your funeral, what are the character qualities he or she would name when thinking back on your life?

2. After reflecting on the list in the above question, are there qualities you would want to add to the list? Are there qualities you would want to subtract?

3. What can you begin doing *today* to bring more of these Short List characteristics into your life?

4. Finally, what was the most significant truth you learned in the entire book? What difference will it make in your life?

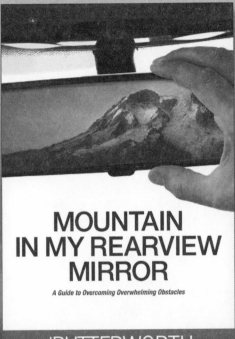